ECHOES OF THE
REFORMATION

FIVE TRUTHS THAT
SHAPE THE CHRISTIAN LIFE

BRANDON D. SMITH

LifeWay Press®
Nashville, Tennessee

Published by LifeWay Press® · © 2017 The Gospel Coalition

ISBN 978-1-4300-5532-7 · Item 006104398

Dewey decimal classification: 248.84
Subject headings: REFORMATION \ CHRISTIAN LIFE \ DISCIPLESHIP

Unless indicated otherwise, Scripture quotations are taken from The Holy Bible, English Standard Version® (ESV®), copyright © 2001 by Crossway, a publishing ministry of Good News Publishers. Used by permission. All rights reserved. Scripture quotations marked CSB® are taken from the Christian Standard Bible®, Copyright 2017 by Holman Bible Publishers. Used by permission.

To order additional copies of this resource, write to LifeWay Resources Customer Service; One LifeWay Plaza; Nashville, TN 37234-0113; fax 615.251.5933; call toll free 800.458.2772; order online at *lifeway.com;* email *orderentry@lifeway.com;* or visit the LifeWay Christian Store serving you.

Printed in the United States of America

Groups Ministry Publishing · LifeWay Resources · One LifeWay Plaza · Nashville, TN 37234-0152

PRODUCTION TEAM

AUTHOR
BRANDON D. SMITH

MANAGER, SHORT-TERM STUDIES
BRIAN DANIEL

ART DIRECTOR
JON RODDA

CONTENT EDITOR
JOEL POLK

PRODUCTION EDITOR
DAVID HANEY

DIRECTOR, GROUPS MINISTRY
MICHAEL KELLEY

TGC EXECUTIVE DIRECTOR
BEN PEAYS

TGC EDITORIAL DIRECTOR
COLLIN HANSEN

VIDEO PRODUCER & DIRECTOR
DAVID WATSON

CONTENTS

HOW TO USE THIS STUDY

This Bible study provides a guided process for individuals and small groups to explore the five *alone* statements that came out of the Reformation and to discover the practical implications of those statements for believers today. This study is divided into the five *alone* statements, along with an introductory week that will provide a good foundation for understanding these Reformation tenets. Here are the topics you and your group will examine together:

1. WHY THE REFORMATION MATTERS
2. SCRIPTURE ALONE
3. GRACE ALONE
4. FAITH ALONE
5. CHRIST ALONE
6. GLORY TO GOD ALONE

One week of Bible study is devoted to each of these topics, and each week is divided into three sections of personal study:

1. THE BIG IDEA
2. DIGGING DEEPER
3. GOSPEL APPLICATION

In these sections you'll find biblical teaching and interactive questions that will help you understand and apply the teaching.

In addition to the personal study, six group sessions are provided that are designed to spark gospel conversations around brief video teachings. Each group session is divided into three sections:

1. **START** focuses participants on the topic of the session's video teaching.
2. **WATCH** provides key ideas presented in the video and space to take notes.
3. **DISCUSS** guides the group to respond to and apply the video teaching.

TIPS FOR LEADING A SMALL GROUP ═══

PRAYERFULLY PREPARE

Prepare for each group session with prayer. Ask the Holy Spirit to work through you and the group discussion as you point to Jesus each week through God's Word.

REVIEW the weekly material and group questions ahead of time.

PRAY for each person in the group.

MINIMIZE DISTRACTIONS

Do everything in your ability to help people focus on what's most important: connecting with God, with the Bible, and with one another.

CREATE A COMFORTABLE ENVIRONMENT. If group members are uncomfortable, they'll be distracted and therefore not engaged in the group experience.

TAKE INTO CONSIDERATION seating, temperature, lighting, refreshments, surrounding noise, and general cleanliness.

At best, thoughtfulness and hospitality show guests and group members they're welcome and valued in whatever environment you choose to gather. At worst, people may never notice your effort, but they're also not distracted.

INCLUDE OTHERS

Your goal is to foster a community in which people are welcome just as they are but encouraged to grow spiritually. Always be aware of opportunities to include and invite.

INCLUDE anyone who visits the group.

INVITE new people to join your group.

ENCOURAGE DISCUSSION

A good small-group experience has the following characteristics.

EVERYONE PARTICIPATES. Encourage everyone to ask questions, share responses, or read aloud.

NO ONE DOMINATES—NOT EVEN THE LEADER. Be sure your time speaking as a leader takes up less than half your time together as a group. Politely guide discussion if anyone dominates.

NOBODY IS RUSHED THROUGH QUESTIONS. Don't feel that a moment of silence is a bad thing. People often need time to think about their responses to questions they've just heard or to gain courage to share what God is stirring in their hearts.

INPUT IS AFFIRMED AND FOLLOWED UP. Make sure you point out something true or helpful in a response. Don't just move on. Build community with follow-up questions, asking how other people have experienced similar things or how a truth has shaped their understanding of God and the Scripture you're studying. People are less likely to speak up if they fear that you don't actually want to hear their answers or that you're looking for only a certain answer.

GOD AND HIS WORD ARE CENTRAL. Opinions and experiences can be helpful, but God has given us the truth. Trust Scripture to be the authority and God's Spirit to work in people's lives. You can't change anyone, but God can. Continually point people to the Word and to active steps of faith.

KEEP CONNECTING

Think of ways to connect with group members during the week. Participation during the group session is always improved when members spend time connecting with one another outside the group sessions. The more people are comfortable with and involved in one another's lives, the more they'll look forward to being together. When people move beyond being friendly to truly being friends who form a community, they come to each session eager to engage instead of merely attending.

ENCOURAGE GROUP MEMBERS with thoughts, commitments, or questions from the session by connecting through emails, texts, and social media.

BUILD DEEPER FRIENDSHIPS by planning or spontaneously inviting group members to join you outside your regularly scheduled group time for meals; fun activities; and projects around your home, church, or community.

ABOUT THE AUTHOR

BRANDON D. SMITH works with the Christian Standard Bible at LifeWay Christian Resources and teaches theology at various schools. The author of *Rooted: Theology for Growing Christians* and *They Spoke of Me: How Jesus Unlocks the Old Testament*, Brandon also cohosts the *Word Matters* podcast. He holds a BA in biblical studies from Dallas Baptist University and an MA in systematic and historical theology from Criswell College. He's pursuing a PhD in theology at Ridley College in Melbourne, Australia. Brandon lives near Nashville, Tennessee, with his wife, Christa, and their two daughters, Harper and Emma.

VIDEO CONTRIBUTORS

KEVIN DEYOUNG, pastor, University Reformed Church; East Lansing, Michigan

R. ALBERT MOHLER JR., president, The Southern Baptist Theological Seminary; Louisville, Kentucky

TREVIN WAX, Bible and reference publisher, LifeWay Christian Resources; Nashville, Tennessee

ABOUT THE GOSPEL COALITION

The Gospel Coalition is a fellowship of evangelical churches deeply committed to renewing our faith in the gospel of Christ and to reforming our ministry practices to conform fully to the Scriptures. We have become deeply concerned about some movements within traditional evangelicalism that seem to be diminishing the church's life and leading us away from our historical beliefs and practices. On the one hand, we're troubled by the idolatry of personal consumerism and the politicization of faith; on the other hand, we're distressed by the unchallenged acceptance of theological and moral relativism. These movements have led to the easy abandonment of both biblical truth and the transformed living mandated by our historical faith. We not only hear of these influences but also see their effects. We've committed ourselves to invigorating churches with new hope and compelling joy, based on the promises received by grace alone through faith alone in Christ alone.

We believe that in many evangelical churches a deep and broad consensus exists about the truths of the gospel. Yet we often see the celebration of our union with Christ replaced by the age-old attractions of power and affluence or by monastic retreats into ritual, liturgy, and sacrament. Any replacement for the gospel will never promote a mission-hearted faith anchored in enduring truth that works itself out in unashamed discipleship eager to stand the tests of Kingdom calling and sacrifice. We desire to advance along the King's highway, always aiming to provide gospel advocacy, encouragement, and education so that current and next-generation church leaders are better equipped to fuel their ministries with principles and practices that glorify the Savior and do good to those for whom He shed His life's blood.

We want to generate a unified effort among all peoples—an effort that's zealous to honor Christ and multiply His disciples, joining in a true coalition for Jesus. Such a biblically grounded and united mission is the only enduring future for the church. This reality compels us to stand with others who are stirred by the conviction that the mercy of God in Jesus Christ is our only hope of eternal salvation. We desire to champion this gospel with clarity, compassion, courage, and joy, gladly linking hearts with fellow believers across denominational, ethnic, and class lines.

Our desire is to serve the church we love by inviting all our brothers and sisters to join us in an effort to renew the contemporary church in the ancient gospel of Christ so that we truly speak and live for Him in a way that clearly communicates to our age. As pastors, we intend to do this in our churches through the usual means of His grace: prayer, ministry of the Word, baptism and the Lord's Supper, and the fellowship of the saints. We yearn to work with all who seek the lordship of Christ over the whole of life with unabashed hope in the power of the Holy Spirit to transform individuals, communities, and cultures.

WHY THE REFORMATION MATTERS

SESSION 1

START

Welcome to group session 1 of *Echoes of the Reformation*. Open the group session by asking participants to introduce themselves with quick answers to the following questions.

What's your name, and what's one thing you're looking forward to this week?

Would you describe yourself as a type A personality (organized, proactive) or a type B personality (easygoing, a dreamer)? Why?

How does your personality type affect your daily life positively and negatively?

Most people fall into one of these two camps. If you're type A, you probably enjoy following a Bible-reading plan or a list of practical steps laid out in your pastor's sermon. If you're type B, you probably have a hard time following a strict Bible-reading plan or to-do list. Instead, you enjoy praying and reading more spontaneously. If we're honest, each personality type thinks the other can be a little crazy.

The truth is, following Jesus is a struggle for all of us. Sometimes we're so caught up in following a step-by-step rule book that we forget to sit back and enjoy the goodness of the gospel. Others of us can be too undisciplined, forgetting that following God requires intentional effort. No matter where you are on this scale, the message of the Reformation is that the gospel brings you back to center, where your life is defined only by the truth of Scripture. You're not your personality type.

Read together as a group Galatians 2:20. Then watch video session 1.

WATCH ═══════════════════════

WHY CONSIDER THE CORE TRUTHS OF THE REFORMATION?

1. It's our history.
2. It's God's truth.

Luther's great joy was in having other people hear the gospel and find their joy in Christ.

Instead of being self-directed, repentance is Christ-directed.

FIVE *SOLAS*

1. Scripture alone
2. Grace alone
3. Faith alone
4. Christ alone
5. Glory to God alone

The word *alone* is important because we are still prone to the same errors.

These foundational truths are meant to bear the fruit of joy in our lives.

DISCUSS

On the video Albert Mohler, Kevin DeYoung, and Trevin Wax discussed the Reformation's impact on Christians today.

Why do you think the Reformation is still important today?

How did the video discussion challenge your view of church history?

Christians in Martin Luther's day didn't have immediate access to Scripture. Their only exposure to Scripture came through the Roman Catholic Church and its leaders. In other words, people couldn't read God's truth for themselves.

Why is it important for believers to read Scripture for ourselves?

Why is it important for believers to focus on the *alone* aspect of the core truths of the Reformation?

The Roman Catholic Church taught that people could find grace in the Church's sacraments and in human works. However, Luther emphasized the necessity of personal repentance and looking to the cross for salvation.

In what ways do you struggle with repentance? Why do you struggle this way?

Close in prayer, thanking God for inviting us to participate in the long history of His redemption of all things.

Complete the following three personal-study sections before the next group session. One section will focus on the big idea, the next section will dig a little deeper, and the final section will focus on gospel application.

THE BIG IDEA

The time for silence is past, and
the time to speak has come.[1]
MARTIN LUTHER

The young, newly ordained Roman Catholic priest stood in front of the church to officiate his first mass. Priests were expected to have clean hearts before officiating. No sin unconfessed. No heart of stone unturned.

But as Martin Luther began to recite the introductory portion of the mass, with the bread and the wine on the altar in front of him, he almost passed out. "I was utterly stupefied and terror-stricken. ... Who am I, that I should lift up mine eyes or raise my hands to the divine Majesty?"[2]

Luther's fear wasn't misplaced. He knew he was a sinner, and he knew he couldn't live up to the cleanliness required of a Catholic priest. Who could? And two other events in his life didn't help either. First, when he had decided to become a priest rather than a lawyer, his father was furious. Luther wouldn't see him again until his ordination day—the day he officiated his first mass. His dad, who finally showed an ounce of support for his new path in life, was sitting in the crowd. No pressure!

Second, Luther had experienced a close encounter with death just a few years earlier. He had been torn between what his parents wanted, what he wanted, and where God's will entered that equation. While heading back to the university after visiting his parents, Luther was nearly struck by lightning. To him this was no accident; he believed it was God's judgment.[3] Luther had been running away from ministry, and God wanted to get his attention. Luther cried out in panic, vowing to become a priest if God spared his life. So he went headfirst into ministry, but he was always haunted by his sinfulness and unworthiness.

Read Proverbs 3:5-6. Have you ever experienced a moment when you weren't sure whether God approved of your decision? How did you respond?

As you look back on that moment, in what ways was God faithful, even in your uncertainty?

THE ACCIDENTAL REFORMATION?

On October 31, 1517—a decade after his ordination as a priest—Luther nailed his now famous 95 Theses to the door of the All Saints' Church in Wittenberg, Germany. Of all these 95 affirmations and concerns, the main point was simple: you can't buy God's grace, and you can't override the authority of the Bible. The Roman Catholic Church had missed these truths, and that was a dangerous place to be.

The Church had begun selling indulgences, certificates from the Church guaranteed to reduce the punishment of sins. As Luther saw it, money was also corrupting everyone in power. On top of that, the Church taught that the pope could receive direct revelation from God—that he had the same authority as the Bible itself. These problems and more pushed Luther to the edge. Like any good leader, he took action. Like any good pastor, he cared for his people. He stepped out when no one else would.

It's important to understand that Luther wanted to reform the Church, but he didn't want to spark a divisive reformation. He wasn't trying to start a new denomination. He was just trying to be faithful to God's Word. As he once said, "I ask that men make no reference to my name; let them call themselves Christians, not Lutherans."[4] But his convictions were strong, and his concerns were legitimate. The gospel compelled him to ignore the dangers associated with stepping out in faith, even when the road wasn't going to be easy. Proclaiming the truth meant more to him than the backlash he would receive for defending it.

If you had been in Luther's situation, how would you have handled it?

Read 1 Peter 3:13-17. Mark a point on the scale to indicate your readiness to defend your faith.

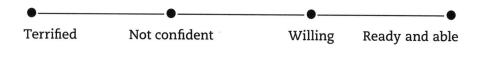

Terrified   Not confident   Willing   Ready and able

How does the gospel free you from fear?

Luther wasn't spreading his theses around in little gospel tracts. He wasn't shouting his complaints from rooftops or using some sort of medieval Facebook to tell his friends how angry he was. By nailing his letter to the church's door, he was actually inviting debate in a way common for his time.[5] He wanted to discuss the truths of the Bible with others. He wanted truth to reign. If they were right, Luther thought, they would demonstrate it by proving him wrong.

But Luther was a bold personality. Don't let his trembling first-mass incident fool you. He was a brilliant theologian and philosopher with a witty and pointed sense of humor. By 1518 his controversial writings began to pick up steam. His issues with the Church's teaching were gaining popularity. He was beginning to transform from frustrated priest to budding revolutionary. And the Church wasn't happy about it.[6]

Luther appeared on trial in 1521 at the Diet of Worms. This had nothing to do with eating worms, by the way. Worms was a town in Germany, and a diet was an assembly held by the leaders of the Holy Roman Empire. At Worms Luther was asked to defend himself. His response summed up the spirit of the Reformation:

> *I am bound by the Scriptures I have quoted and my conscience is captive to the Word of God. I cannot and I will not recant anything, since it is neither safe nor right to go against conscience.*[7]

Luther was never formally punished for his battles against the Church because he fled Wittenberg. While in hiding, he most notably translated the entire New Testament into German. In 1521 the Diet of Worms reached a decision declaring that Luther was a heretic and that no one should follow his teachings. Unfortunately for the Church—but fortunately for us—his influence couldn't be suppressed. The Reformation had begun.

THE AFTERMATH OF THE REFORMATION

From 1521 to 1522, while Luther was in hiding, he began writing letters to people back home, and they wrote back telling him stories of freedom. Monks were marrying nuns, monks were filling in their bald spots with hair, and people in the churches began taking communion themselves.

While these actions may seem normal to us, they were madness to the Roman Catholic Church. Luther celebrated these freedoms but warned against letting this liberty become more about clothes, diet, and haircuts than about worshiping God.[8] Luther wanted people to have freedom to worship God as He's revealed in Scripture and to understand salvation through Christ alone. Nothing more, nothing less.

Luther returned from hiding in late 1521 to find fellow Reformers pillaging Catholic parishes and vandalizing icons to Mary, carrying knives while they did it. Luther quickly reminded his followers that he didn't seek to create a violent insurgence. "Preach, pray, but do not fight,"[9] he warned. He saw his work as faithfulness to Scripture, not a war on the Roman Catholic Church. He didn't set out to destroy; he set out to reform. God's people aren't to treat their freedom like a badge of honor; rather, they're to obey God's freeing Word. Luther returned to Wittenberg to convince believers of just that. He wanted them to find their identity in nothing but Christ alone.

What freedoms in your life interrupt instead of enhance your worship of God?

REFORMING OUR HEARTS

Even Christians are prone to wrap up our identities in things other than Jesus Christ. For Luther, it was first his father's approval. He wanted to be a priest, but his father wanted him to be a lawyer. This was the greatest identity crisis of Luther's life, and it nearly wrecked him.

But then Luther had another identity crisis—one all Christians can relate to. He knew God had called him to be a priest, and he embraced that calling. But beyond his priestly robe, Luther was a sinner in need of grace. His sin tortured his soul much more than a bad sermon ever could have. And when he went to the pages of Scripture, he realized that he couldn't buy God's grace. God's grace was a free gift.

I identify myself as a husband, a dad, and a writer. All of these roles are truly parts of who I am, and I love being all of them. But those identities are temporary, limited to this earthly life. In eternity I'm a child of God. That's my true identity. And that's your true identity. As we discussed in the group session, we aren't our personality type. That might be a part of the way God wired us, but it doesn't define us. Personality type or any other human attribute can become a crutch more than a set of wings.

We must go to Scripture with confidence that we'll find there the truth about our identity. We must recognize that sin is costly, but grace is free. We must join Luther in proclaiming, "I am bound by the Scriptures I have quoted and my conscience is captive to the Word of God." In our unbelief we must quote one of Luther's favorite passages, Mark 9:24: "I believe; help my unbelief!"[10] May God define us, nothing else.

Spend a few moments praying Mark 9:24: "I believe; help my unbelief!" Ask God for help in forsaking anything that stands in the way of the truth of His Word.

1. Martin Luther, as quoted in Stephen J. Nichols, *The Reformation: How a Monk and a Mallet Changed the World* (Wheaton, IL: Crossway, 2007), 37.
2. Martin Luther, as quoted in Roland H. Bainton, *Here I Stand: A Life of Martin Luther* (Nashville: Abingdon, 1978), 25.
3. Carl R. Trueman, *Luther on the Christian Life: Cross and Freedom* (Wheaton, IL: Crossway, 2015), 32.
4. Martin Luther, as quoted in Eric W. Gritsch and Robert W. Jenson, *Lutheranism: The Theological Movement and Its Confessional Writings* (Philadelphia: Fortress, 1976), vii.
5. Trueman, *Luther on the Christian Life*, 38.
6. Ibid., 39.
7. Martin Luther, as quoted in *Documents from the History of Lutheranism, 1517–1750*, ed. Eric Lund (Minneapolis: Fortress, 2002), 32.
8. Bainton, *Here I Stand*, 195.
9. Martin Luther, as quoted in Bainton, *Here I Stand*, 204.
10. Timothy J. Wengert, *Reading the Bible with Martin Luther: An Introductory Guide* (Grand Rapids, MI: Baker Academic, 2013), 62.

DIGGING DEEPER

This is the gospel, that sins are remitted in the name of Christ;
and no heart ever received tidings more glad.[1]
HULDRYCH ZWINGLI

When I first became a youth pastor, I was young and impressionable. The pastor who had mentored and later hired me could have pushed me in a wrong direction, but he didn't. He formed me as a pastor to be loving, self-sacrificing, honest, and ethical. He didn't let me get away with anything less, because he loved the church too much to see it abused or hurt by its leaders. I worked with him for only a year, but his impact on my life and ministry still provides the core of who I am as a ministry leader.

In the same way, the Reformation didn't end when Martin Luther died in 1546. Its impact is still felt today. Most obviously, if you're a Protestant (that is, not Roman Catholic or Eastern Orthodox), you're a product of the Reformation. We stand on the shoulders of Christians in the past, and knowing where we came from will help us keep moving forward on the mission to which God has called us.

As we discussed earlier, Luther's greatest legacy to us is his love for and submission to Scripture. Because he loved Scripture, he aligned his life with it. He wasn't perfect—no one is!—but his love for the gospel, rooted in Scripture, should be an inspiration to us. He acted on what he believed.

In reading about Luther in the first section of this week's study, did you relate to any of his struggles or successes? Which ones?

Read James 2:18-19. What was James's point in making this dramatic comparison?

Think of a time when you acted in a way that didn't reflect what you said you believed. What was the problem?

THE CLOUD OF WITNESSES

Since we are surrounded by so great a cloud of witnesses, let us also lay aside every weight, and sin which clings so closely, and let us run with endurance the race that is set before us, looking to Jesus, the founder and perfecter of our faith, who for the joy that was set before him endured the cross, despising the shame, and is seated at the right hand of the throne of God.
HEBREWS 12:1-2

These "witnesses" (v. 1), introduced in Hebrews 11, are people who came before us and experienced both peace and suffering for their faith. The writer of Hebrews wanted readers to understand that those Christians laid a foundation that still matters today.

Let's look at some of these witnesses in Hebrews 11.

ABEL was faithful to God, and his faithfulness was "a more acceptable sacrifice" (v. 4) than his brother Cain's. Abel offered an acceptable blood sacrifice, while Cain merely offered fruit. Cain eventually became the world's first murderer, killing Abel in a jealous rage. Yet Hebrews declares, "through his faith, though [Abel] died, he still speaks" (v. 4). His sacrifice for God—which ended up costing him his life—is an example to us today.

NOAH did as God had commanded and built an ark, though he didn't fully know why. Yet Noah was faithful to God's command, being motivated by "reverent fear" (v. 7). His desire to follow God was more important than his own ego.

ABRAHAM was willing to lay his own son, Isaac, on the altar and sacrifice him (sound familiar?) to follow God's commands. God spared Isaac's life because, as the Hebrews writer said, "He considered that God was able even to raise him from the dead, from which, figuratively speaking, he did receive him back" (v. 19). Abraham's faith was so strong that not even the death of his son would shake his faith that God was powerful and good.

The writer went on to mention many others who both conquered kingdoms in God's name and were killed for God's name. In every circumstance "all these, though commended through their faith, did not receive what was promised" (v. 39). God blessed all these people, but they didn't get to meet Jesus—the ultimate promise they all looked forward to.

So we cling to the cross, knowing we're blessed to be right here in this time, on the other side of Jesus' sacrifice. We've benefited from the faith of so many before us, from Abel to Noah to Luther, and we've also received the greatest benefit of personal faith in Christ. This large cloud of witnesses stands in heaven, their faith spurring us on as examples.

> **Name the person who has influenced your life the most. Why did he or she have such an impact on you?**

> **Record the name of one person you can influence for the gospel and ways you can intentionally disciple him or her.**

TRUTH IN A WORLD OF OPPOSITION

Luther understood that the falsehood being taught by the Roman Catholic Church was detrimental to the lives of people around him. The witnesses of Hebrews 11 understood that faith in God offered a greater hope than their current circumstances. Their lives help us realize that opposition is no match for the gospel.

It's common today to hear remarks like "How can we know what truth really is?" and "How dare you tell me that your truth is better than my truth!" Many people accuse anyone with biblical convictions of being intolerant, hateful, and exclusive. It's not considered loving, after all, to tell people they should change their beliefs.

Consequently, it's tempting to take the easy road nowadays. If you stay out of the way, you're less likely to be insulted, picketed, or even ignored. Instead, we agree with those who say, "We should just love everyone! Your truth is yours; my truth is mine." This would have been an easy sentiment for Luther or others in the Bible, like Jesus' disciples.

In Acts 5 the apostles were teaching about Jesus in the temple courts right after being released from prison for doing just that. They ran into trouble with the authorities again, and they were arrested and brought before the religious leaders. When told never to preach again, they argued that doing so would disobey God. They were beaten and released, again warned not to preach the gospel again. Their response?

> They left the presence of the council, rejoicing that they were
> counted worthy to suffer dishonor for the name. And every day,
> in the temple and from house to house, they did not cease teaching
> and preaching that the Christ is Jesus.
> **ACTS 5:41-42**

Read Acts 5:21-42. Notice that the apostles weren't angry or hostile, even though they didn't shy away from their convictions. Why did they remain calm?

Think of an example from your life when you faced opposition for your faith. How did you respond?

How does the gospel make us hopeful even in the face of opposition and potential hardship?

BELIEF IN ACTION

Though we shouldn't seek out a punch to the face or a whip across the back, the faith of the apostles, the Reformers, and everyone who lived in between is the same faith we have today. They weren't super-Christians who were called to something more godly than we are. God used them to reform their times, and God can use us to reform ours today.

The first step is for us to know what we believe and why we believe it. That's why those who came before us were willing to do anything and go anywhere for the mission of God. They realized that you can't separate belief from action. You do what you believe.

For Luther and the Reformers, belief in action sometimes meant losing the things they loved. For Luther, it was first his relationship with his father, and later it was his ministry in the Roman Catholic Church. For those in the Bible, belief in action often meant physical or emotional suffering. And yet they're our heroes in the faith, and their joy outweighed their grief. Like the pastor I served alongside early in ministry, they laid a foundation that we can continue to build on. Church history, from the New Testament and beyond, is a crucial component of our lives of faith today.

How did you feel about church history before reading this lesson?
□ I hadn't thought much about it.
□ I thought it was interesting but not important to my life.
□ I viewed Christians from church history as inspirations to my faith.

How has learning some of the history behind the Reformation changed the way you view what you believe?

List three lessons you learned from the life of Luther and the story of the Reformation.

1.

2.

3.

Another Reformer, Huldrych Zwingli, famously said:

> *This is the gospel, that sins are remitted in the name of Christ;*
> *and no heart ever received tidings more glad.*[2]

May we stand for the gospel regardless of our circumstances, knowing that nothing makes our hearts more glad than proclaiming the good news that first came to us by the proclamation of the faithful believers who went before us.

We'll finish our study this week by looking at five core truths that came out of the Reformation, truths that still echo today. Those core truths will form the basis for the next five weeks of our study as we look at the important beliefs of the Christian faith and why they matter in our lives.

Spend a few moments in prayer, asking God to make you bolder in your faith in both word and deed.

1. Huldrych Zwingli, as quoted in James R. Payton Jr., *Getting the Reformation Wrong: Correcting Some Misunderstandings* (Downers Grove, IL: IVP Academic, 2010), 120.
2. Ibid.

GOSPEL APPLICATION

We should not investigate what the Lord has left hidden in secret …
nor neglect what he has brought out into the open, so that we
may not be convicted of excessive curiosity on the one hand,
or of excessive ingratitude on the other.[1]
JOHN CALVIN

Belief in action. This idea has been repeated a lot this week, but we haven't fully discussed what we should believe. What beliefs from Scripture form the basis for the ways we love God and others?

When the core truths that came out of the Reformation are defined, they're usually expressed in the form of *solas*. The word *sola* is the Latin word for "alone" or "only." The five *solas* are *sola scriptura* ("by Scripture alone"), *sola gratia* ("by grace alone"), *sola fide* ("through faith alone"), *solus Christus* ("through Christ alone"), and *soli Deo gloria* ("glory to God alone").

These terms weren't coined by Luther or any of the Reformers, though Reformers used them in various ways. Instead, they've more recently become the way to describe the DNA of the Reformation. As we'll see, they're more than a bunch of cold Latin terms that academics throw around in church-history books. The five *solas*, like the Reformation itself, are intensely practical. They're grounded in a real-life, everyday following of Jesus. They're the most important, basic biblical truths you can ever believe.

Look at the five *solas* again and read Ephesians 2:4-5. How do these verses summarize the truths behind the *solas*?

God, being rich in mercy, because of the great love with which
he loved us, even when we were dead in our trespasses, made
us alive together with Christ—by grace you have been saved.
EPHESIANS 2:4-5

Which statement describes you more accurately?
☐ I know more facts about the Bible than I actually live out day to day.
☐ I'm all about action but can't always articulate what I believe.

FAITH SEEKING UNDERSTANDING

Belief is an interesting thing. Everyone believes in something, right? Not just normal beliefs like the grass is green or the sky is blue. Everyone believes in deeper truths, like goodness, beauty, love, and purpose.

Christian beliefs go even further. We don't believe in a generic, watered-down version of God the way the world sees Him. We confess and believe certain things about God that affect how we understand everything in life.

As we've already said, we do what we believe. According to Paul in Romans 10:9, what we confess with our mouths and believe in our hearts is a matter of salvation, of eternity. The 95 Theses were a clarion call for the Roman Catholic Church to reform some of its beliefs because it directly influenced people's lives, not just immediately but forever.

An example we discussed earlier this week is the selling of indulgences. People could buy certificates from the Church in exchange for the promise of less punishment for their sins in the afterlife. Someone might say, "Jesus is the only One who can take away the punishment for sins, so who cares whether people thought indulgences accomplished something for them? They seem kind of harmless, right?"

But in reality, these indulgences minimized wholly trusting in Christ for salvation by adding human works. Christians don't mix false beliefs with right beliefs. Scripture is our authority, and we believe what it teaches. So we don't give God 99 percent worship and throw in a few indulgences just in case. It's slavery to believe that anything other than God can forgive sins and erase the punishment for them. The Church in Luther's day was selling grace, but the Bible teaches that grace is free. You can't buy it, not even from the Church.

Remember, God isn't calling us to an ignorant faith. Scripture is an inexhaustible treasure chest of God-centered, life-changing truth. Our faith shouldn't be blind. It should continually seek more and more understanding about the glorious God we serve. We should center our lives on the key truths He has laid out for us. And that's where the five *solas* come in.

Read James 1:22-25. How do these verses enrich this week's discussion?

THE REFORMATION ECHOES TODAY

Let's finish this week with a brief summary of each of the *solas* we'll study over the next five weeks. Go back and read the quotation by John Calvin at the beginning of this lesson. God is so infinite, so extraordinary, that we can't know everything to be known about Him. Our minds can't contain it. But we're often greedy, wanting to know just a little more than He has chosen to give us.

On the other hand, God has been unbelievably kind to reveal Himself to us and has allowed us to know Him in a personal, loving way. Sometimes we want to focus on what we don't know rather than be thankful for all He has invited us to know, so we take for granted what He has shown us in Scripture. But if we never learn another thing about God or His work in our lives, these five *solas* would be more than enough. They still echo in our world and our lives today if we're willing to listen.

SOLA SCRIPTURA: SCRIPTURE ALONE

> *All Scripture is breathed out by God and profitable for teaching,*
> *for reproof, for correction, and for training in righteousness, that*
> *the man of God may be complete, equipped for every good work.*
> **2 TIMOTHY 3:16-17**

The teaching of the Roman Catholic Church in Luther's day didn't mesh well with this Scripture. The Church claimed that the teaching of the pope had the same authority as the teaching of the Bible. The pope, in a very real sense, had as much power as Scripture. But Paul told Timothy that Scripture is from God and makes Christians "complete" (v. 17). It's not Scripture plus the pope, nor is it Scripture plus anything else. Scripture alone is all we need to learn about God and teach others about God.

Why can no one—not the pope or your pastor or Brother Joe next door—be on a par with God's Word?

SOLA GRATIA: GRACE ALONE

*Sin will have no dominion over you, since
you are not under law but under grace.*
ROMANS 6:14

Grace is most easily defined as "unmerited favor." God gives grace because
He's loving and merciful, not because we deserve it. It's free. Absolutely,
positively free. We're saved by grace alone.

The Roman Catholic Church couldn't sell grace, and Luther knew this.
Indulgences put an unbearable law on God's people. The Church said, "Do
this and do that, buy this and buy that, and God will give you grace when
it's time to be punished for your sins." Talk about pressure!

But God in His Word tells us that we've got no shot of earning grace.
And that's OK, because Jesus came to earth as walking, talking grace. That
fact shows us that we could never get grace on our own.

**How often do you try and earn God's grace through good deeds
and hard work?**

Never   Rarely   Sometimes   All the time

SOLA FIDE: FAITH ALONE

*By grace you have been saved through faith. And this is not your own doing;
it is the gift of God, not a result of works, so that no one may boast.*
EPHESIANS 2:8-9

This verse shows grace and faith together. The fact that we even have faith
is a gift of grace! God didn't have to give us faith. He could have pulled the
plug on His whole plan after Adam and Eve sinned, leaving us to wander
in the dark. But He didn't.

We're justified—declared to be right with God—through faith alone. This *sola* is perhaps the cornerstone of the Reformation. Luther's struggle with his own sin, his continual feeling of being an absolute wretch, reminded him that faith was all he had. He couldn't offer anything else. Knees on the ground, palms in the air—he had faith that God saved him, and that was his only hope.

Why is it important to understand that faith is a gift from God rather than something we've mustered ourselves?

SOLUS CHRISTUS: CHRIST ALONE

Jesus said to him, "I am the way, and the truth, and the life. No one comes to the Father except through me."
JOHN 14:6

There's no Christianity without Christ. Real shocker, I know. But sometimes, when we're caught up in ourselves or even our churches and ministries, we forget that we don't own Christianity. We're on Christ's mission; He's not on ours. There's no grace without Christ. There's no faith without Christ. Frankly, there's no Scripture without Christ, for Scripture is about Him (see John 5:39).

Luther saw the Roman Catholic Church abusing its power, taking Christianity away from Christ. In his eyes the Church had put the pope in place of Christ. He once said, "You are not lords over the pastoral office. ... You have not instituted the office, but God's Son alone has done so."[2] When it comes to salvation, Christ alone. And when it comes to church leaders, even though they're are supremely important to the church (see Heb. 13:17), Christ alone.

Why is the idea of Christ alone an unpopular message today, even sometimes among Christians?

SOLI DEO GLORIA: GLORY TO GOD ALONE

The heavens declare the glory of God,
and the sky above proclaims his handiwork.
PSALM 19:1

We noted earlier that *sola fide* might be the cornerstone of the Reformation. If that's the case, *soli Deo gloria* might be the mortar that holds the stones together. As one theologian has pointed out, the Roman Catholic Church in Luther's day didn't deny the importance of Scripture, grace, faith, and Christ in salvation. But if you asked about "the little word *alone,* we would soon find genuine disagreement."[3]

God's glory alone? Well, the Church ran into a bigger problem here. God can't have all the glory if people play any part in salvation. And the Church insisted that works are an essential part of salvation, not just an outflow from it. Luther rightly fought against this thinking. God gets all the glory, not us. We're just blessed to be able to look up and see the heavens declaring His glory.

God's glory describes His perfect character and the reason
He receives praise and credit for all things. Record three ways
you try to share glory with God.

1.

2.

3.

Spend a few moments in prayer, asking God to help you believe
rightly so that you can live rightly.

1. John Calvin, as quoted in Timothy George, *Theology of the Reformers,* rev. ed. (Nashville: Broadman & Holman Publishing Group, 2013), 242.
2. Martin Luther, as quoted in George, *Theology of the Reformers,* 102.
3. David VanDrunen, *God's Glory Alone: The Majestic Heart of the Christian Faith and Life* (Grand Rapids, MI: Zondervan Academic, 2015), 14.

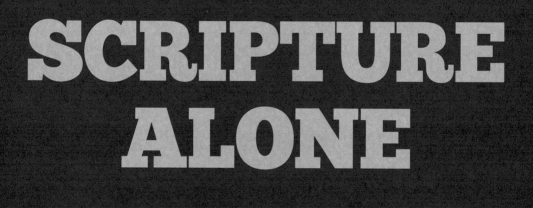

SCRIPTURE ALONE

SESSION 2

START

Welcome to group session 2 of *Echoes of the Reformation*. Last week we were introduced to the background of the Reformation, most notably through the life of its catalyst, Martin Luther. Answer these questions as you reflect on last week's study.

In what ways did Martin Luther's story encourage you this week?

Faith in action was a key principle for Luther. How did you put your faith in action this week?

At any time in any period of history, people can look around the world and see that things aren't as they should be. Sin is an age-old enemy, and its weapons take many forms. Christians and non-Christians alike see that death, destruction, pain, grief, and brokenness form the foundation of almost every news story. The world is so broken that closing your eyes and plugging your ears are about the only ways to miss that fact.

And yet if we're honest, we know we can't just shut the world out and avoid sin, because it lives deep inside each of us. We can move into a shack in the middle of the woods with no connection to the outside world, and we'll still have a roommate—the sin in our hearts. Praise God, His Word tells us that all isn't lost. Through Jesus Christ and by the power of the Holy Spirit, God is healing all that's broken.

This week we'll turn our eyes and hearts to Scripture. Watch video session 2 with your group.

WATCH

It's not that the Bible is the only authority that we ever look to, but it is the final authority. It has the last word.

This is God speaking to us, living and active.

Sola Scriptura was the doctrine that led to all the other affirmations of the Reformation.

Sola Scriptura was a direct statement that the papacy is not a conduit of revelation. Scripture alone is.

Luther and the Reformers believed that Scripture alone can reach the human heart.

The Word of God is sufficient to do the work of God.

The Scripture does require something else, and that's the ministry of the Holy Spirit.

DISCUSS

On the video Albert Mohler, Kevin DeYoung, and Trevin Wax discussed the idea of *sola scriptura*—Scripture alone.

Why do you think this doctrine is still important today?

How did the video discussion challenge your view of Scripture?

If the Bible is truly God's Word, then it carries God's authority. To believe in Scripture alone is to believe God's Word has the final say in your life.

Why is it important to believe the Bible is more than a normal book?

In what ways do you struggle to look at God's Word as the final authority for your life?

The Roman Catholic Church taught that Scripture was one authority alongside the Church's leadership. Today people still think submitting to the Bible's authority is silly or naïve, but they actually find the authority for their lives in a variety of sources.

If your words, thoughts, and actions reflect what you believe about Scripture's authority in your life, how much authority does Scripture have over you? Why?

1——2——3——4——5——6——7——8——9——10
No authority   Total authority

Close in prayer, thanking God for giving us His Word.

Complete the following three personal-study sections before the next group session.

THE BIG IDEA

What is asserted without the Scriptures or proven revelation may be held as an opinion, but need not be believed.[1]
MARTIN LUTHER

Reading the Bible was the primary spark in Luther's transformation from Roman Catholic monk to revolutionary. As we saw last week, he stood before the leaders of the Church and proclaimed:

I am bound by the Scriptures I have quoted and my conscience is captive to the Word of God. I cannot and I will not recant anything, since it is neither safe nor right to go against conscience.[2]

When Luther began to see that the Church's practice wasn't lining up with God's Word, he had a choice to make: suppress his conscience or listen to it. As an aspiring priest and preacher, he felt the weight of being faithful to God's Word. He once wrote:

It is a glory which every preacher may claim, to be able to say with full confidence of heart: "This trust have I toward God in Christ, that what I teach and preach is truly the Word of God."[3]

Luther didn't view Scripture's authority as merely a piece of the Christian puzzle or as an important but not an ultimate doctrine; it was the concrete slab on which the Christian house stood. For him, the preacher's primary task was to preach God's Word rightly because of its sheer power and unchangeable truth. So when the pope exercised authority apart from Scripture or in contradiction to Scripture, Luther would have none of it. Scripture plus anything else equaled truth mixed with error.

How have you responded to the misuse of power, either in your own life or elsewhere?

Why should we submit to God's authority above all other claims of authority?

THE AUTHORITY OF SCRIPTURE

All Scripture is breathed out by God and profitable for teaching, for reproof, for correction, and for training in righteousness, that the man of God may be complete, equipped for every good work.
2 TIMOTHY 3:16-17

Paul's words sum up the authority of Scripture; it's inspired, "breathed out" (v. 16), by God. The very words of God sit on the pages of Scripture. The same breath that brought the world into existence and filled Adam's lungs with life is the same breath that formed Scripture.

Saying Scripture is the ultimate authority falls on rocky soil in today's world. Authority comes with all kinds of baggage. Abuse, coercion, force, and manipulation run rampant when people exercise power. Even in a democracy like America, our votes don't always turn out the way we want, and the leaders we elect don't always prove to be trustworthy.

Perfect authority seeks to bring peace and create a flourishing society, and most of us know this. So when leaders are crooked and let us down, we're angry. We know in our hearts that God, the ultimate authority of the universe, isn't that type of leader. His Word isn't an edict from a high castle to keep the peasants in line, and His Word isn't an agenda to step on others' heads so that He can climb to the top of the mountain. His Word, instead, is for our good. God wants us to know Him and His will. Who better to know than our own Creator?

What does 2 Timothy 3:16-17 say about the origin and authority of Scripture?

If your words, thoughts, and actions reflect what you believe about Scripture's authority in your life, how much authority does Scripture have over you?

1————2————3————4————5———— 6————7————8————9————10
No authority   Total authority

How can you allow the Bible to have more authority in your life?

If God is the ultimate authority, the good and true King, then His words are good and true. He's perfect, so His Word is perfect. His commands are right, and our obedience to them is right. No pope or president or self-help book can outweigh what God has to say to us. And no matter what a leader does, even the pope, God's Word has the final say.

For Luther, the Bible's truthfulness wasn't about putting its claims into a petri dish and observing whether it passed the test. He didn't need a pope or a scientist to authenticate its claims. He trusted Scripture because he trusted God. Believing in the authority of God's Word takes action. The Word of God is alive, and it's ready and able to change your life, if only you'll submit to its authority as Luther sought to.

THE WORD IS ALIVE

The word of God is living and active, sharper than any two-edged sword, piercing to the division of soul and of spirit, of joints and of marrow, and discerning the thoughts and intentions of the heart. And no creature is hidden from his sight, but all are naked and exposed to the eyes of him to whom we must give account.
HEBREWS 4:12-13

The Reformation caused a massive split in the global church. Protestants (literally, "the protesters") were born. And Protestants are a people of the Bible first and foremost. In the Bible we find who God is and ways He relates to His people. Following in the footsteps of Luther, Protestants believe when Scripture speaks, God speaks.

If we believe nothing else, we should believe this: God's Word is alive. The Bible isn't an outdated, crusty book that fits better on a shelf than in our laps. No, it sits there rumbling like an earthquake, holding the life-changing words of the God of the universe. It's applicable to your life now. Today. And tomorrow too.

If we believe Scripture is truly the Word of God, we'll believe what it says. Like Luther, we'll believe a doctrine is true only if it's found in the Bible. In the coming weeks we'll look at the most important truths to come out of the Reformation, but we should first take a look at reforming our hearts. We must be open to growing before we can actually grow.

Read again Hebrews 4:12-13. Circle the words that describe God's Word.

Why is it important to recognize these characteristics of Scripture?

THE KING HAS SPOKEN

To Luther, the pope was more like a bad king than a good pastor. He abused his power and sought to control the people. The Word of God no longer controlled the Roman Catholic Church; its leader did. A church with a minimized Word is not a church at all; it's a train without tracks, a winding mountain road without guardrails.

The danger for us is to try and become kings ourselves, trying to assert our own authority rather than turning to God and His Word for wisdom. Some of us want to be the king of our workplace or the king of our home. Some of us want to be the king of our fantasy-football league or the king of our neighborhood's Christmas-light displays. Some of us treat the highway as our own little kingdom, demanding that our minions ask our permission before they change lanes or slow down.

Kings stand above everyone else, receiving praise and reverence from everyone around them. Nothing is withheld from kings, after all. They never come in second place, and they never have to acquiesce to another's needs. Kings have the power to fix stuff, including their own lives. It's good to be a king.

In what ways do you try to control your own life?

Record three ways trying to take control of your life has backfired.
I.

2.

3.

Now record three ways giving control to God has blessed you.
I.

2.

3.

We're always either wanting to be king or looking to imperfect people to lead us perfectly. Our kings never fulfill us. We look outwardly in our culture or inwardly to ourselves, but we rarely look to the King we already have. And we rarely turn to His Word to glean the truth He's left there: God is King, and you aren't—and that's a good thing.

The King of the universe is perfect. He's just, loving, merciful, and full of grace. He doesn't barter with lesser kings, He can't be bribed, and He's not corruptible. He doesn't just do good; He is good. Luther was repulsed by those—like himself!—who claimed to have control over the things only God had control over. Calling himself a "stupid clod," he cautioned against presuming "wisdom and power for ourselves."[4]

Though we live in constant revolt, lobbing grenades at His doorstep, God loves and leads. Luther was always amazed by this truth. God doesn't smite us. He doesn't send us into exile, as the Church dismissed Luther. He still welcomes us to His table. We can still approach His throne boldly (see Heb. 4:16) through prayer and through Scripture.

God never intended for us to make up our own rules or go our own way. He's a King who gave us, in His Word, the best marching orders ever given. He's a King who didn't merely send orders from His throne but walked into battle for His people in the person of Jesus Christ. His death was the death of death; His victory was our victory; His kingdom is our kingdom. He's the King we need because He's the king we can never be, never find, and never elect. Our search was over before it began. He's the answer to every question. He's the King we're longing for and the King we already have.

Spend a few moments thanking God for His revealed Word to us. Pray that He will help you see that His Word is enough for every need in life.

1. Martin Luther, as quoted in Timothy George, *Theology of the Reformers*, rev. ed. (Nashville: Broadman and Holman Publishing Group, 2013), 81.
2. Martin Luther, as quoted in *Documents from the History of Lutheranism, 1517–1750*, ed. Eric Lund (Minneapolis: Fortress, 2002), 32.
3. Martin Luther, *Martin Luther's 95 Theses and Selected Sermons* (Jersey City, NJ: Start Publishing, 2012).
4. Martin Luther, as quoted in Stephen J. Nichols, *The Reformation: How a Monk and a Mallet Changed the World* (Wheaton, IL: Crossway, 2007), 37.

DIGGING DEEPER

Get thee to God's Word.[1]

WILLIAM TYNDALE

Blockbuster superhero movies and the latest iteration of the *Star Wars* movie franchise show the power of a good story. Grown men and young children alike dress up in costumes, stand in line for hours, and spend $62 on a bucket of popcorn just to watch larger-than-life heroes do the unthinkable. People are riveted by a good story that seems otherworldly, and they're willing to scrounge up the money and time to invest if they're convinced they'll enjoy it.

In my work with the Christian Standard Bible, I came across research from the Barna Group stating that people don't read the Bible for a few reasons but primarily because they don't have enough time or struggle to relate to the language. The stats showed that 88 percent of American households own a Bible, but only 37 percent of people read it once a week or more.[2] No doubt their frustration with trying to understand words, phrases, and concepts in Scripture is a reasonable frustration. However, as most preachers have told their congregations, people have plenty of time to read, but they simply don't want to make the time.

In an average week how often do you read the Bible, aside from Sunday morning at church?
☐ **Less than once**
☐ **Once**
☐ **More than once**

List three reasons you don't read the Bible as often as you would like.
1.
2.
3.

WHY DON'T WE READ THE BIBLE?

Let's assume Barna is right—that we don't want to make time to read our Bibles. Why don't we? I mean, the God of the universe has given human-kind His Word. He could have given up on us when we disobeyed Him in the garden, but He didn't. He didn't let us hide from him; He went looking for us and spoke to us (see Gen. 3). God spoke to Luther through His Word during a time of the church's status quo, and it led to a positive change in the church. As we'll see, He still speaks to us today when we open His Word and open our hearts and minds to its words. Isn't that enough?

Frankly, it isn't enough for most of us. We revere and even worship God, and we surely think the Bible is valuable. But the foundational reason we don't read it regularly is that we don't understand how Scripture works. We think God left a Book behind thousands of years ago as a trail of bread crumbs to help us find Him, but we don't give it much more credence than that. We treat the Bible like a wise old man who left us inspirational stories from long ago but is a little out of touch with the basic struggles of our contemporary lives. We fail to see the unbridled power it possesses.

Identify a point on the scale to indicate your reliance on God's Word for wisdom and instruction.

Never   Rarely   Sometimes   All the time

Are you more prone to turn to God's Word only in times of trouble or because you genuinely want to meet God there?

In the end our struggle with Bible reading is often not because of time or effort or ability but because we don't expect to meet God there. We know at some level that God spoke in His Word, but we don't fully understand that He still speaks to us through His Word. In short, we don't know what happens to us when we read it. We don't understand how God works on us through His Word.

Luther understood the Bible's power to change lives because the Bible changed his own life. His reading of Romans 1:17 changed the course of his life, and he was never the same. Not only that, but he also loved the Word so much that he dedicated years of his life to translating the New Testament into German, his native language. When it was published in 1522, he was elated that people "might seize and taste the clear, pure Word of God itself and hold to it."[3] Luther thought the Bible was more important than any book anyone could ever savor. The Roman Catholic Church at the time didn't allow massive access to the Bible. Most people knew only what the priests told them. But Luther knew that God had met him in its pages, and he longed for others to have that access.

WHAT HAPPENS WHEN WE READ THE BIBLE?

Learning from Luther, we shouldn't merely open the Bible and read it the way we read any other book. Nor should we set aside time to read the Bible because we want to be entertained in the same way a movie would entertain us. Instead, we should read the Bible as an assent to the basic function of Scripture.

Let's revisit some foundational passages we've already discussed. Paul told Timothy:

> *All Scripture is breathed out by God and profitable for teaching,*
> *for reproof, for correction, and for training in righteousness, that*
> *the man of God may be complete, equipped for every good work.*
> **2 TIMOTHY 3:16-17**

Notice the verbs: "Scripture is breathed out by God and profitable" (v. 16). They're active verbs that emphasize Scripture's relevance for today, not verbs describing a distant time when God's Word meant something to ancient people. Pair these verses with the powerful text in Hebrews:

The word of God is living and active, sharper than any two-edged sword, piercing to the division of soul and of spirit, of joints and of marrow, and discerning the thoughts and intentions of the heart. And no creature is hidden from his sight, but all are naked and exposed to the eyes of him to whom we must give account.
HEBREWS 4:12-13

Again notice that the Word of God is living, effective, and able to judge the ideas and thoughts of the heart. If Jesus is the Word of God (see John 1:1) and He's not dead, then the power of God's Word on the pages of Scripture isn't dead either. If the Holy Spirit speaks through the Word (see 2 Pet. 1:21), the Bible still has a heartbeat. The Word is alive! Luther interpreted Scripture as something that was applicable to him that day, at that time. The Roman Catholic Church wasn't obeying God's Word, and the Bible told Luther so.

Before reading this lesson, how would you have described the Bible?

What gives Scripture its power today, in the here and now? How does its power affect the way you approach Scripture?

Reread Tyndale's quotation at the beginning of this section of study. How can you set up avenues in your life to get to the Word?

As a captive to God's Word, Luther was led by the Holy Spirit to understand important truths about theology and the Christian life. Today, through the illumination of the Holy Spirit, our spiritual eyes are opened to the supernatural, life-giving truth of God's living Word too. When we open its pages, the Bible speaks to us and calls on us to "taste and see that the LORD is good" (Ps. 34:8). The Bible, in a real sense, admits us to the mind of God:

> As it is written,
> "What no eye has seen, nor ear heard,
>   nor the heart of man imagined,
> what God has prepared for those who love him"—
> These things God has revealed to us through the Spirit. For the Spirit searches everything, even the depths of God. For who knows a person's thoughts except the spirit of that person, which is in him? So also no one comprehends the thoughts of God except the Spirit of God. Now we have received not the spirit of the world, but the Spirit who is from God, that we might understand the things freely given us by God. And we impart this in words not taught by human wisdom but taught by the Spirit, interpreting spiritual truths to those who are spiritual.
> **1 CORINTHIANS 2:9-13**

Want to know what God thinks? Open your Bible. The Holy Spirit lives in you to help you understand God's will and character, to help you taste and see something fresh and new that you've never seen before. A passage you read five years ago might speak to you differently today because the living God speaks to you through His living Word right here and right now.

THE GREATEST STORY EVER TOLD

> Let nobody suppose that he has tasted the Holy Scriptures sufficiently unless he has ruled over the churches with the prophets for a hundred years.[4]
> **MARTIN LUTHER**

This quotation reminds us that we'll never fully exhaust the Word of God. It's a diamond we can see and appreciate but never fully excavate. Its words tell a story like none other. *Star Wars* is great. Superhero movies are spellbinding. But they're all copies; they're lesser stories of a greater story. God's Word will captivate us like those stories only when we realize that God meets with us on its pages. We'll agree with John Calvin that our thoughts and words should be conformed to Scripture, where God Himself speaks.[5]

We need God to speak to us, but we don't always believe He does. If Scripture is good for training us in righteousness, then we recognize where to turn to know the Righteous One and to be trained in righteousness. I need God's Word. You need God's Word. We need God's Word. Scripture is true, powerful, and relevant. Let's pray for God to make its truth, its power, and its relevance real to us.

Spend the next few moments asking God for a hunger and thirst for His Word. Acknowledge to Him that His Word is living, active, and applicable to your life today.

1. William Tyndale, as quoted in Timothy George, *Theology of the Reformers,* rev. ed. (Nashville: Broadman & Holman Publishing Group, 2013), 340.
2. Barna Group, "The State of the Bible, 2014," [online, cited 15 November 2016], 9, 11. Available from the Internet: *americanbible.org/uploads/content/state-of-the-bible-data-analysis-american-bible-society-2014.pdf*.
3. Martin Luther, as quoted in Michael Reeves, *The Unquenchable Flame: Discovering the Heart of the Reformation* (Nashville: B&H Academic, 2009), 55.
4. Martin Luther, as quoted in George, *Theology of the Reformers,* 105.
5. Charles Partee, *The Theology of John Calvin* (Louisville: Westminster John Knox, 2008), 68.

GOSPEL APPLICATION

No condemnation now I dread;
Jesus, and all in Him, is mine!
Alive in Him, my living Head,
And clothed in righteousness divine,
Bold I approach the eternal throne,
And claim the crown, through Christ my own.[1]
CHARLES WESLEY

When I was an elementary-school kid, my family moved around a lot. My favorite place we lived was an apartment complex in the heart of the Dallas-Fort Worth metroplex. A busy road ran right alongside those apartments, and my parents forbade me to cross it. The thing is, across the road was a little gas station that had all the candy a sweet-toothed kid like me could ever want. My parents wanted what was best for me, but I wanted immediate gratification.

One afternoon a few other kids and I decided that we would make a run for it. One of my friends, Corey, stayed back. He was more afraid of getting into trouble than the rest of us. After making a few jokes at his expense, we crossed the road.

Just a few minutes later, as I stood in line with a friend who actually had the money to buy something, I looked over and recognized my dad's light-washed jeans. I looked up, and sure enough, he was standing there. He had been around the corner as my friends and I jeered at Corey before we sprinted to that candy heaven where we now stood. He was smirking at me, probably because the sheer terror in my eyes must have been pretty funny. I didn't get a spanking that day, because my dad decided my fear was punishment enough. But I learned a lesson: my dad was always watching.

While my dad seemed to be everywhere all the time, our Father in heaven really is. He's always there, pressing us to obey Him, to follow Him, to treasure Him, and to trust Him. As we discussed in the previous lesson, he speaks truth to us in His Word, but we don't always want to listen. We would rather run across a busy street than simply stay where He asks us to stay and partake of what He has to offer us.

> **Reflecting on what you've read about Scripture so far, list three reasons the idea of Scripture alone is so crucial to Christian living.**
>
> 1.
>
> 2.
>
> 3.

THE WORD DOES IT ALL

> *I simply taught, preached, and wrote God's Word; otherwise I did nothing. …*
> *The Word so greatly weakened the papacy that never a prince or emperor*
> *did such damage to it. I did nothing. The Word did it all.*[2]
> **MARTIN LUTHER**

This quotation illustrates that God's Word gripped Luther. As we've already examined, Scripture itself led Luther to question the Roman Catholic Church of the day. The Word absolutely floored him, and yet he didn't observe the same reverence for the Word in his own Church tradition. The pope exercised similar, if not the same, power over Christians as the Bible did.

What's interesting is that, in the end, Luther took no real credit for the Reformation. He didn't ask for a plaque or a gold-plated watch. Instead, he said, "The Word did it all." As Kevin DeYoung said on the video, "The Word of God does the work of God." Luther dropped the mic and let the Word speak for itself. This was something the Church didn't understand.

Now consider this truth alongside our discussion in the previous lesson about God's Word being alive, working today as it did yesterday and the day before that. If Scripture works by the power of the Holy Spirit, then the work continues. So when we look at Luther's words, we understand that the truth of God's living and active Word did far more than Luther ever could have. God Himself was at work.

The Bible isn't just another book. It's not a dust magnet, a doorstop, or a paperweight. As Psalm 33 proclaims:

> *By the word of the LORD the heavens were made,*
> *and by the breath of his mouth all their host.*
> **PSALM 33:6**

The Bible has power because Almighty God spoke it into existence the same way He spoke creation into existence. So not even a great theologian like Luther could hold a candle to the raw power of God's Word.

Why was Luther so insistent on giving credit to God's Word for the reforms he advanced?

How often do you take credit for something God has done?

Never   Rarely   Sometimes All the time

TAKING THE WORD TO OTHERS

The following passage is one of the first descriptions of Christians gathering together after Jesus' resurrection:

> *They devoted themselves to the apostles' teaching and the fellowship, to the breaking of bread and the prayers. And awe came upon every soul, and many wonders and signs were being done through the apostles. And all who believed were together and had all things in common. And they were*

selling their possessions and belongings and distributing the proceeds to all, as any had need. And day by day, attending the temple together and breaking bread in their homes, they received their food with glad and generous hearts, praising God and having favor with all the people. And the Lord added to their number day by day those who were being saved.
ACTS 2:42-47

God had just sent the Holy Spirit in His fullness, and these Christians were beginning to understand what it meant to follow Christ after His ascension. The passage describes living in community, being generous, and radically influencing the lives of others. People were coming to know Christ daily, just by being in the presence of these believers. But why were these Christians' lives making such an impact? The beginning of the passage tells us: "They devoted themselves to the apostles' teaching" (v. 42). And what were the apostles teaching? God's Word.

Now to be clear, these apostles didn't have leather-bound Bibles in their hands, reciting passages of 1 Corinthians or Hebrews, but their sermons were no doubt based on Jesus' teachings and on the Old Testament, which would all later become solidified in the Bible we now hold in our hands. Though they faced prison and worse, they immediately began broadcasting the Word of Christ and the good news of the gospel.

Jesus commissioned the apostles to share His Word with the world (see Matt. 28:18-20). Although Acts tells us they were suffering persecution for doing so, why did they continue to preach His Word?

Record at least one way sharing God's Word might cause a struggle or interference in your day-to-day life.

God's Word empowered the early believers to lead sacrificial, others-centered lives. These believers shared their possessions with one another and hosted traveling Christians in their homes. Doubtless, they struggled with pride and selfishness much the way we do, but God's Word was their final authority, and it demanded that they walk the Calvary Road of selflessness.

Being sacrificially generous is difficult. Sharing our possessions and inviting people into our homes can be exhausting. These early Christians no doubt struggled with the same sins of pride and selfishness as we do, but they let God's Word have the final say.

THE WORD AND THE ENDS OF THE EARTH

As we've noted, Luther didn't preach the truth of God's Word in order to cause division. On the contrary, he wanted to bring the church together under the authority of Scripture. He wanted the church to stay together, reading the Bible together and submitting to it. He wanted the leaders of the church to be like the apostles—devoted to God's Word alone. No additives. No substitutes.

The gospel is the greatest unity we can offer because it saves anyone and everyone who believes it, bringing believers into the same body of Christ. It offends, yes, but it also unites. Like Luther and like the early Christians in Acts, we should be emboldened by the power of God's Word to take the gospel to our living rooms, our neighborhoods, and to the ends of the earth. We shouldn't have dinner with Sally next door to show her how righteous we are, trying to make her more like us. Rather, we should show her the character of Christ and the truth of God's Word.

How often do you find yourself apologizing for or minimizing what the Bible says?

What keeps you from believing that God's Word does the work, not you?

List three ways you can point to God's Word rather than yourself in your life and in your relationships with others.

Luther took no credit for the church-shaping, gospel-advancing Reformation, so surely we can't take credit for any work we're doing for God's kingdom. The Word does it all. Saying Scripture alone is our final authority isn't a cop-out; it's confidence. Because of sin we're fragile people. We can't save anyone. We can't be Jesus to anyone. But we can point people to the beauty of God's Word and to the life, death, and resurrection of Christ portrayed in its pages. We aren't confident in ourselves, but we're supremely confident in God and in the power of His Word.

CROSSING THE STREET

I ran across the street next to my apartment complex, not because I was commanded to but because I wanted to. I was told not to, but I wanted to be accepted by my friends. I wanted the candy waiting for me inside that gas station even though I didn't have any money to actually buy it. Who said sin is logical?

We've all made illogical sacrifices for our own gain. We'll take a chance if we think they'll bring us enjoyment. Luther sacrificed everything to proclaim the Word of God. Are we willing to do the same? Will we follow the example of the early Christians and sacrificially love others for the sake of the gospel? Paul reminds us in 2 Corinthians 12:7-10 that we're weak. We don't tell the gospel from a position of strength but from a position of trust in the power of God's Word to do its work in drawing sinners to Christ.

Spend the next few moments asking God to change your heart through His Word and to give you the desire and strength to take His truth to others.

1. Charles Wesley, "And Can It Be," as quoted in Michael Reeves and Tim Chester, *Why the Reformation Still Matters* (Wheaton, IL: Crossway, 2016), 38.
2. Martin Luther, as quoted in Timothy George, *Theology of the Reformers*, rev. ed. (Nashville: Broadman & Holman Publishing Group, 2013), 55.

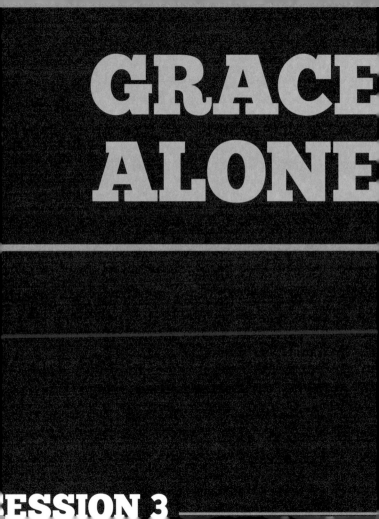

GRACE ALONE

START

Welcome to group session 3 of *Echoes of the Reformation*. Last week we examined the idea that Scripture alone is our authority. Answer this question as you reflect on last week's study.

In what ways did your reading of God's Word change during or after last week's study?

The hymn "Grace Greater than Our Sin," written in 1910, has been well known and (mostly) well sung for more than a hundred years. If you know the tune, sing this as a group or say the words aloud together.

Marvelous grace of our loving Lord,
Grace that exceeds our sin and our guilt,
Yonder on Calvary's mount outpoured,
There where the blood of the Lamb was spilt.

Refrain:
Grace, grace, God's grace,
Grace that will pardon and cleanse within;
Grace, grace, God's grace,
Grace that is greater than all our sin.

Dark is the stain that we cannot hide;
What can avail to wash it away?
Look! There is flowing a crimson tide;
Brighter than snow you may be today.
(Refrain)

Marvelous, infinite, matchless grace,
Freely bestowed on all who believe;
All who are longing to see His face,
Will you this moment His grace receive?
(Refrain)[1]

This week we'll take a look at the marvelous grace of God. Watch video session 3 with your group.

WATCH

Grace is God's unmerited favor.

The righteousness of Christ is imputed to our account. It's reckoned to be ours though we do not possess it in our own behavior and life.

God is not an earthly father. He is the holy and righteous God, whose righteousness we can't possibly meet in any sense.

The problem with merit is that it doesn't exist. All that really exists is the sheer grace and mercy of God.

God demands an absolute righteousness. That's what He provided in His own Son.

We are not saved by the setting aside of justice but by the fulfillment of justice.

The cross is not only the demonstration of God's great love for us, but it's also the demonstration of the seriousness with which He took sin.

Because we are part of God's family, there's an extraordinary responsibility and calling that come with this.

DISCUSS ════════════════

On the video Albert Mohler, Kevin DeYoung, and Trevin Wax discussed the idea of *sola gratia*—grace alone.

Why do you think this doctrine is still important today?

How did the video discussion challenge your view of grace?

The Reformers saw in Scripture that there's no such thing as grace plus works. If we could work for our salvation, we wouldn't have needed Christ to die on the cross, rise from the dead, and impute His righteousness to us.

Why is it important that grace is unmerited?

Why is the assertion of works-based salvation bad news, not the good news of the gospel?

The Roman Catholic Church taught that people could earn or receive grace through works, the purchase of indulgences, and even suffering in purgatory. The Reformers, however, insisted that these teachings cheapened the truth of grace.

In what ways do you try to earn God's grace or favor?

Close in prayer, thanking God for giving us His grace.

Complete the following three personal-study sections before the next group session.

1. Julia H. Johnston, "Grace Greater than Our Sin," in *Baptist Hymnal* (Nashville: LifeWay Worship, 2008), 105.

THE BIG IDEA

We are beggars: this is true.[1]
MARTIN LUTHER

You might be surprised to know that Luther taught salvation by grace alone while he was a Roman Catholic monk—and it wasn't all that controversial.[2] However, *grace alone* didn't mean what Luther would eventually mean by this term. The Church taught that grace didn't save completely but rather prepared people to be saved. Luther the monk said grace alone is the gasoline that propels the car of salvation. Luther the Reformer said grace alone is the entire car.

Luther's view of grace alone became biblical as he moved away from the man-made traditions of the Roman Catholic Church. He later commented on the shift in his teaching:

> It's true. I was a good monk and kept my order so strictly that I could say that if ever a monk could get to heaven through monastic discipline, I should have entered in. All my companions in the monastery who knew me would bear me out in this. For if it had gone on much longer, I would have martyred myself to death, what with vigils, prayers, readings, and other works. ... And yet my conscience would not give me certainty, but I always doubted and said, "You didn't do that right. You weren't contrite enough. You left that out of your confession." The more I tried to remedy an uncertain, weak and troubled conscience with human traditions, the more daily I found it more uncertain, weaker and more troubled.[3]

Much like Paul in Philippians 3, Luther followed all the rules and kept all the doctrines of the Church. But rules don't save us; grace does. True grace is found in Christ, not in personal morality and strength. Here's a segment of Paul's story:

I myself have reason for confidence in the flesh also. If anyone else thinks he has reason for confidence in the flesh, I have more: circumcised on the eighth day, of the people of Israel, of the tribe of Benjamin, a Hebrew of Hebrews; as to the law, a Pharisee; as to zeal, a persecutor of the church; as to righteousness under the law, blameless. But whatever gain I had, I counted as loss for the sake of Christ.

PHILIPPIANS 3:4-7

In what ways do you treat God's grace like an additional benefit rather than all-sufficient?

How is your story similar to Paul's?

GRACE UPON GRACE

From his fullness we have all received, grace upon grace. For the law was given through Moses; grace and truth came through Jesus Christ.

JOHN 1:16-17

You may recall from week 2 that Luther was keenly aware of his sin. In the end he couldn't serve in his priestly duties because he felt so unworthy of God. He knew he needed grace. Big-time.

In contrast, the Roman Catholic Church was trying to sell grace to people. Through indulgences and other goods they were wrapping up grace with a nice bow on top, creating a sort of Roman Catholic Supermarket for God's grace. Luther knew he needed grace, and he also knew grace came only from God. The Church had no right to charge for something God gave freely. He said:

Do we work nothing for the obtaining of this righteousness? I answer: Nothing at all. For the nature of this righteousness is, to do nothing, to hear nothing, to know nothing whatsoever of the law or of works, but to know and to believe this only, that Christ is gone to the Father and is not now seen: that he sitteth in heaven at the right hand of his Father, not as a judge, but made unto us of God, wisdom, righteousness, holiness and redemption.[4]

The Roman Catholic Church taught that even the works people performed (or bought) were still a matter of God's grace.[5] Luther wanted no part of that. Grace plus works doesn't equal grace. Christ came into the world, died on the cross, and went back to heaven because we can't earn grace. How could grace truly be unmerited favor if a person could earn it? Jesus would have stayed at home if we could play a part in our salvation.

Before this lesson how did you view grace versus works?

Why was it so important for Luther to distinguish between works and grace?

Luther and the Reformers realized that teaching people to work harder or to pay higher prices for grace isn't the gospel. After all, *gospel* means "good news." And we all know from experience that we're hopelessly lost without the grace of God. We sin every day. Telling us to be perfect would be bad news. Really, really bad news.

The truth is, we're all on the same playing field: "All have sinned and fall short of the glory of God" (Rom. 3:23). The nicest person you've ever met and the most hateful person you've ever met have one big thing in common: without God's grace they're without hope.

THE GOOD NEWS OF GRACE

All have sinned and fall short of the glory of God,
and are justified by his grace as a gift, through
the redemption that is in Christ Jesus.
ROMANS 3:23-24

The previous passage is one of the most beloved and memorized passages in the Bible. Why? Probably because we all resonate with it. We all sin. Every single day. Because we sin, we're unlike our perfect God; we fall short of His glory. But through grace we're justified; we're declared right in God's eyes. God looks at you through the lens of His Son, Jesus Christ, hanging on the cross and walking out of the grave.

If we're honest, we know that all we bring to salvation's table is sin—pride, lust, anger, selfishness, hatred, idolatry—and none of this can be served at what the Bible calls "the marriage supper of the Lamb" (Rev. 19:9). Everyone who believes in Christ will attend this meal, and only His righteousness will get us a seat.

Record three ways you've experienced God's unmerited grace in your life.

1.

2.

3.

When you received this grace, were you quick to thank God for it? Why or why not?

I often meet Christians who believe salvation is by grace through faith in Jesus, but they live as if living the Christian life is all up to them. They believe God has saved them, but they don't live like it. As Paul wrote in Galatians 3:3, we're foolish if we think God's work in our life, which began by the work of the Holy Spirit, can be completed in our own strength. The Holy Spirit begins the work and completes it, all by grace. As Paul tells us:

> *In him you also, when you heard the word of truth, the gospel*
> *of your salvation, and believed in him, were sealed with the*
> *promised Holy Spirit, who is the guarantee of our inheritance*
> *until we acquire possession of it, to the praise of his glory.*
> **EPHESIANS 1:13-14**

Grace isn't an optional, take-it-or-leave-it type of belief. It's the power, the mercy, of God that saves us. The Holy Spirit, God Himself, lives in us to guarantee that we're sealed in Him. Grace won't leak out every time we sin. It won't eventually leave us. If anything, it will overflow within us. God saves us by grace, grows us by grace, and brings us into eternity by grace.

THE DELIVERING GRACE OF CHRIST

> *If Christ be made guilty of all the sins which we all have committed,*
> *then are we delivered utterly from all sins, but not by ourselves,*
> *nor by our own works or merits, but by him.*[6]
> **MARTIN LUTHER**

The Son of God stepped into our world to bring salvation. It's sheer grace that He came to us at all. He didn't have to. We didn't even ask Him to. But God is a God of grace through and through. Grace is given freely, not begged for or bought.

On the cross grace flowed from the veins of Jesus as His blood was poured out for us. Our sins nailed Him there, and His grace kept Him there until His last breath. But it didn't stop there. He walked out of the grave three days later and sent the Holy Spirit to seal our salvation. His grace never dries up. In love God pours His grace into us in the person of His Spirit.

Imagine a salvation built on works. Imagine reading Romans 3:23 and then being told you need to be good to be saved. Imagine reading Ephesians 1:13-14 and then being told a scrap of paper can seal your salvation. What an epic letdown. But thanks be to God, His grace doesn't let us down.

Moving forward, in what ways can you be more aware of God's grace in your life?

Spend the next few moments thanking God for the sufficiency of His grace and identifying ways you'll respond to His good and free gift.

1. Martin Luther, as quoted in Carl R. Trueman, *Luther on the Christian Life: Cross and Freedom* (Wheaton, IL: Crossway, 2015), 195.
2. Michael Reeves and Tim Chester, *Why the Reformation Still Matters* (Wheaton, IL: Crossway, 2016), 81.
3. Martin Luther, as quoted in Reeves and Chester, *Why the Reformation Still Matters*, 84.
4. Martin Luther, *Martin Luther: Selections from His Writings*, ed. John Dillenberger (New York: Anchor, 1962), 105.
5. Timothy J. Wengert, *Reading the Bible with Martin Luther: An Introductory Guide* (Grand Rapids. MI: Baker Academic, 2013), 85–86.
6. Martin Luther, as quoted in Dillenberger, *Martin Luther: Selections from His Writings*, 138.

DIGGING DEEPER

*As soon as the grace of Christ begins to prevail
in any one, the reign of sin and death ceases.*[1]
JOHN CALVIN

Most times my wife and I get into a disagreement, I shoot for the quick fix. I want to talk about it immediately and resolve the issue as quickly as possible. This usually goes well; we say we're sorry, and we move on. To my wife's credit, she's an even-tempered and forgiving woman. But other times she needs more time to think, reflect, or simply cool down. Still other times I don't take my own advice. I pout and wait for her to seek reconciliation with me.

External conflict like this was one result when sin entered the world. In the first story of humankind's existence, sin immediately created blame shifting and strife between our ancient parents, Adam and Eve (see Gen. 3). The division in their relationship wasn't merely a result of outside forces, though Satan's temptation played a huge part. More than that, their struggle came from within. The sin in their hearts created a deep fault line between God and people and between people and other people. Sin fractured them— and us—at the core (see Rom. 5:12).

Mark the place on the scale that represents your willingness to accept blame in a conflict.

Never   Rarely   Sometimes   All the time

How does grace influence the way you handle conflict with others?

THE GREAT CONFLICT IN OUR HEARTS

> *None is righteous, no, not one;*
> *no one understands;*
> *no one seeks for God.*
> *All have turned aside; together*
> *they have become worthless;*
> *no one does good,*
> *not even one.*
> **ROMANS 3:10-12**

The first point in Luther's 95 Theses says, "Our Lord and Master Jesus Christ, in saying 'Do penance …,' wanted the entire life of the faithful to be one of penitence."[2] The Roman Catholic Church in Luther's day saw penance (or the more familiar word, *repentance*) as buying or begging for grace through indulgences or praying to saints who had died. But Luther clarified what Jesus meant when He urged repentance: His people are to live a life of repentance, which is fueled by Him and nothing else.

The grave conflict in our hearts between God and others can't be swept under the rug by a few dollars and an "I'm sorry." It can't be done by mere hard work. As we've discussed, we don't bring anything to the table. God loves and cherishes us as special creatures made in His image, but this doesn't mean we can be God and therefore perfect. A life of repentance—of continually turning from our sin and turning to Jesus—is the by-product of grace, not the cause of it. As Romans 3:10-12 makes clear, no one is righteous. That's why we need the Righteous One. Repentance, then, must be something we do often, pushing away sin, drawing closer to Christ, and allowing His grace to cleanse us from sin.

In an average week how often do you intentionally repent of your sins?
□ **Less than once**
□ **Once**
□ **More than once**

List three reasons you don't repent of a sin you regularly commit.

1.

2.

3.

We live in a world where it's easier to avoid conflict or to hide what's going on deep inside our hearts than it is to acknowledge a problem. We live in a world that tells us to work harder, to be better, to take care of ourselves even if doing so hurts others. We live in a world that tells us to be true to ourselves. We live in a world that tells us that we're fine just the way we are, that we don't need to be rescued. But the world's story lies about how bad the bad news really is.

The gospel gives us something better. The gospel tells us God knows and loves us, so there's no reason to hide. The gospel tells us we're transformed by the work Jesus has already done when He died on the cross and rose again, so there's no reason to live in self-condemnation. The gospel tells us we can love and sacrifice for others, because Jesus loved us and sacrificed His life for us. The gospel tells us being true to ourselves means understanding we're sinners who need grace. The gospel is good news for bad people.

A LIFE OF REPENTANCE

In Luther's time the Roman Catholic Church taught that merits for salvation could be earned or received from the pope and the priests. Christians could build up merits, sprinkle in some grace, and be on the fast track to eternity with God. But did Jesus actually teach this?

In His ministry Jesus made it a point to tell people that He was the only way to God (see John 14:6). He even rebuked the religious leaders of His day for thinking salvation could be found in their own merit or works and for teaching people to live righteously in ways that even the religious leaders couldn't (see Matt. 23:13-39). As Luther recognized, Jesus' teaching and the Church's teaching didn't match up.

On the cross Jesus said, "It is finished" (John 19:30). And He really meant it. Everything that needed to be done, Jesus did. He gave us the gospel to make us new and to continue making us new. He gave us His righteousness and took on punishment for our sins (see Rom. 8:1-4). God knows sin is strong—so strong that it's impossible to defeat it on our own. More than that, sometimes we like to sin. It feels good or gets us what we want in the moment. That's why Jesus finished the work. We don't have to measure up to anything because He has already measured up. We don't have to do anything because Jesus has already done everything.

In what ways do you try to get to God other than through the only way, Jesus?

How often do you try to do the work of pleasing God that Jesus has already done on the cross?

The gospel doesn't simply make you a better person or a person who now has the power to work a little harder at being good. Your life in Christ isn't simply better; it's totally new! Your life isn't about being better, acting better, or believing better advice; it's about understanding how much better Jesus is than anything else in the universe. It's about grace alone changing your life.

Because you've been changed and given a new life, you have an overflowing amount of grace pumping through every fiber of your being. As Albert Mohler said on the video, merit doesn't exist; only the grace and mercy of God exist. The question is never about whether God gives you grace; the question is always about your response to His grace. Will you be prideful or humble? Will you thank Him or accuse Him of holding out on you? Grace is free, and it's a gift you can't improve on. So repent, over and over, in gratitude for His grace.

A GRACE-FULL IDENTITY

Your identity as either a loving mom or an arrogant jerk will one day be gone. All the "good" and "bad" things you've done will pass away. What will stand forever is your identity in Christ and the grace He has given you. Eternity won't be split between good people and bad people. It will be split between those who are standing in the grace of Christ through faith in Him and those who haven't placed their faith in Christ and are standing on the merit of their own effort.

And remember that our merit doesn't add up in some bank account in God's economy. The only thing that counts is Jesus' perfect righteousness, substituted for our sin. Our lives are lives of grace. We should say with Paul, "It is no longer I who live, but Christ who lives in me" (Gal. 2:20). Because God has given us this grace, we live in light of the reality that Christ resides in us and seals us through the Holy Spirit.

How often do you try and earn grace? Mark a point on the scale.

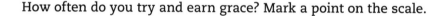

Never   Rarely   Sometimes   All the time

How does God's grace challenge your attempts to earn it?

Our identity is more than our accomplishments, goals, and good morals. It's also more than our sins, struggles, and situations. The gospel tells us on our best day we still needed Jesus to die on the cross for our sins. The

gospel also tells us on our worst day Jesus loved us enough to die for us. Whether we're puffed up with pride or beaten down by frustration, the gospel has something to say to us: were not as good as we think we are, nor are we as hopeless as we think we are.

Paul's transformation from a killer of Christians to an apostle of Christ was radical, but it didn't happen overnight. He never killed another Christian after he met Christ, but life wasn't perfect all of a sudden. Paul told the Corinthians that he still needed to be reminded of grace:

> *To keep me from becoming conceited because of the surpassing greatness of the revelations, a thorn was given me in the flesh, a messenger of Satan to harass me, to keep me from becoming conceited. Three times I pleaded with the Lord about this, that it should leave me. But he said to me, "My grace is sufficient for you, for my power is made perfect in weakness." Therefore I will boast all the more gladly of my weaknesses, so that the power of Christ may rest upon me. For the sake of Christ, then, I am content with weaknesses, insults, hardships, persecutions, and calamities. For when I am weak, then I am strong.*
>
> **2 CORINTHIANS 12:7-10**

We're strongest not when we're standing up to giants but when we're kneeling down before God. Strength—true strength—is found in a life of repentance. Grace knocks us off our feet so that we can sit at the foot of the cross.

Spend a few moments expressing your gratitude for God's grace. Acknowledge that His grace has always been and will always be enough.

1. John Calvin, *St. Paul's Epistle to the Romans*, The John Calvin Bible Commentaries (Altenmünster, Germany: Jazzybee Verlag, 2012).
2. Martin Luther, as quoted in Timothy J. Wengert, *Martin Luther's 95 Theses: With Introduction, Commentary, and Study Guide* (Minneapolis: Fortress, 2015), 13.

GOSPEL APPLICATION

The whole teaching of the Gospel is a sure demonstration that what God has promised will certainly be performed. For the Gospel is now an accomplished fact: the One who was promised to the patriarchs, and to the whole race, has now been given to us, and in him we have the assurance of all our hope.[1]
HULDRYCH ZWINGLI

We've discussed this before, but it bears repeating: the Reformation wasn't merely about Luther's frustration. It also wasn't about little pieces of his theology being at odds with the teachings of the Roman Catholic Church. It was about everyday people like you and me, who were being taught that they didn't have direct access to God or that God's grace wasn't sufficient for them. Luther couldn't stand by and watch the Church shackle people with the bonds of works-based salvation.

When people today are asked how they can get to heaven, they often respond with an answer like "Be a good person. Love others. Treat people the way you want to be treated." That sounds pretty good, doesn't it? The world would be a much better place if everyone lived that way. But even if everyone lived that way, they wouldn't be promised eternity with God.

So when we step out our front doors into the world, what are we telling people about God's grace? Are we living lives that, shaped by the gospel and empowered by the Spirit, reflect God's grace, mercy, and love? If the world believes it can build its own stairway to heaven with steps made of good intentions, how are we giving people better news of salvation by grace alone?

Reflect on what you've read about God's grace so far and list three reasons the idea of grace alone is so crucial to Christian living.
1.

2.

3.

THE GIFT OF GRACE

While they long for you and pray for you,
because of the surpassing grace of God upon
you. Thanks be to God for his inexpressible gift!
2 CORINTHIANS 9:14-15

When we think about the Reformers' work to restore the good news of the gospel to the church, we recognize a high level of unselfishness. Were they perfect? No, of course not! But they were on a mission that was bigger than themselves. When we contemplate grace, we realize that God's mission to save sinners is bigger than us.

God is the giver of all good gifts (see Jas. 1:17). Grace, as Paul said in the previous passage, is indescribable. We can try to describe it. We can talk about the fact that grace is free, that it's unmerited, or that it can't be bought, but we can't fully describe it. It's hard to put into words something that we can't fully grasp. It's truly indescribable.

That said, we shouldn't be afraid to tell others about it. God gives us grace to share the gospel of grace and only requires that we point others toward it.

Who in your life needs to know about God's grace?

In what ways can you demonstrate grace and then tell that person about God's grace in your life?

Grace realized is grace shared with others. Whenever you receive an amazing Christmas present, it doesn't take long for you to break it out of its box and then tell others about it. You're so excited by the gift, how can you keep from talking about it? It's no different for us. The world needs to hear about the good news of grace. There's enough bad news out there.

GRACE IS UNSELFISH

Of the countless ways grace is a gift, it might be most appropriate to say that grace is unselfish. Think about it: God the Father sent his one and only Son into the world to save us (see John 3:16). Grace wasn't just an idea for God; grace had a name. As John 1:14 tells us, Jesus was "full of grace and truth." The Father could have done away with us and kept His Son from dying a gruesome death for our sins. But He didn't.

Showing grace to others doesn't come naturally to us. To the contrary, in our fallen nature we demand grace for ourselves but keep it from others. We aren't perfect, but God is. We can't save anyone, but we can show grace to others by unselfishly giving ourselves. We reflect God's character by being unselfish with our time, energy, money, and resources.

Why are we sometimes reluctant to sacrificially show grace to others?

In what ways can you sacrificially show grace to others the way God has shown sacrificial grace to you?

My three-year-old daughter is much better at saying, "Thank you" than she is at sharing. She gladly receives, but she's not always willing to spread the wealth. When she's selfish, I correct her and tell her why she should share: because God shared the greatest gift, His Son, with us.

Of course, I'm much better at correcting my daughter's selfishness than my own. Just as she quickly forgets someone's kindness to her, I quickly forget God's kindness to me. "Thank God," I'll say. "Now leave me alone so that I can gobble up all this grace for myself!" Yeah, I can act like a three-year-old. I'm far too often selfish with the greatest gift I've ever received.

WHERE GRACE IS FOUND

> *Let us then with confidence draw near to the throne of grace, that we may receive mercy and find grace to help in time of need.*
> **HEBREWS 4:16**

I said at the beginning of this lesson that the world thinks it can find grace in places other than God. Even the Roman Catholic Church in Luther's time taught this. It said the Church had some grace too, if you had the money to pay for it. "Come to church to receive God's grace" doesn't sound so bad, does it? That idea seems harmless or even helpful until the church actually starts thinking grace comes from inside its doors rather than from God Himself.

It's easy for even Christians to accidentally feed others the lie that grace is found in us, in the church, or in good morals. If a person thinks grace is found in drugs, we shouldn't trade that idol for the idol of church attendance. If a person believes being a good person means acting like their sweet aunt Louise, we shouldn't also tell them that being a good person is acting like a Christian. Grace doesn't say, "Trade a good work for a better work," "Clean yourself up," or "Act more Christian." Instead, grace says, "You bring nothing to the table, but Christ has brought everything to the table for you."

Why can we approach the throne of grace "with confidence," according to Hebrews 4:16?

How does our access to God's grace affect our telling others about it?

Christ's work trumps your work. His work gives you rest—eternal, joyful, final rest (see Heb. 4:1-11). It's not knowing the right formula or memorizing the entire Bible. That would mean you've got the right tools to save someone, and you don't. Instead, you have God the Holy Spirit inside you, working through you. Point others to Him—the only source where grace is found.

GRACE PROCLAIMED EVERYWHERE

> *[God] desires all people to be saved and*
> *to come to the knowledge of the truth.*
> **1 TIMOTHY 2:4**

This is a simple statement by Paul to his young apprentice, Timothy. If there's one verse to keep in your mind at all times, it's this one. Why? Because it reminds you that no sinner is beyond God's power to save. Commenting on this passage, Calvin said:

*There is no people and no rank in the world that is excluded from
salvation; because God wishes that the gospel should be proclaimed
to all without exception.*[2]

As I continue to remind you, this was a large part of Luther's problem
with the Church. Grace was for everyone everywhere, but the Church was
holding out on its people, keeping grace inside it walls. The Church didn't
tell people to merely live a life of repentance but rather to complete pre-
scribed works to make sure they were saved. The Church shackled people
with a works-based system that was devoid of the gospel.

Now look at your own life. Do you create a system of works for those
who are far from God or struggling in their faith? Do you tell them to clean
up their lives and straighten up their act? Or indirectly, do you model for
them a life of moral hard work? Others should be amazed by the work of
God's grace in your life, not at the level of discipline you've achieved in
your own strength.

**Spend the next few moments asking God to help you understand
more and more that His grace is meant not only to be received but
also to be shared. Pray that He will help you point others to His
grace because He has given it to you without reservation.**

---

1. Huldrych Zwingli, as quoted in Michael Reeves and Tim Chester, *Why the Reformation Still Matters* (Wheaton, IL: Crossway, 2016), 49.
2. John Calvin, *St. Paul's Epistles to Timothy, Titus and Philemon*, The John Calvin Bible Commentaries (Altenmünster, Germany: Jazzybee Verlag, n.d.).

FAITH ALONE

SESSION 4

START

Welcome to group session 4 of *Echoes of the Reformation*. Last week we discussed the idea that God's grace alone saves us. Answer these questions as you reflect on last week's study.

In what ways did being more aware of God's grace affect your life this week?

In what ways did you show God's grace to others this week?

My wife and I recently had a conversation about being the parents of two young kids. When days are rough, it's easy to try and muster the strength to be good parents. When days are smooth, it's easy to pat ourselves on the backs for being good parents. In both cases, though, we're looking at ourselves for justification.

Yet the gospel provides us with a better narrative. It tells us we're justified—declared to be right with God—by faith in Christ alone. We can't have faith in ourselves. We make terrible saviors. On our best day and our worst day, we still need Christ. It's so easy to forget that simple truth. Pride wants us to look inward for justification. After all, it's pretty easy to justify ourselves since we always think we're right. But the gospel wants us to look up in faith and see Christ, the only One who can truly justify us for eternity.

This week we'll consider the way the truth of grace alone meshes with and flows into the truth of faith alone. Watch video session 4 with your group.

WATCH

Faith is the only instrument by which we can receive all of Christ's benefits.

Faith is a knowledge, an assent, and a trust.

Faith in Christ equals justification, which yields good works.

Christian discipleship is the fight of faith. We never have to leave faith behind.

We have the very great temptation to trust in our own works because we can see them and we can feel good about ourselves when we do them.

At the heart of the Reformation was a desire to have confidence, assurance: Can I really know that God is for me?

Justification by faith alone pointed to the Christian's assurance that we are saved.

DISCUSS

On the video Albert Mohler, Kevin DeYoung, and Trevin Wax discussed the idea of *sola fide*—faith alone.

Why do you think this doctrine is still important today?

How did the video discussion challenge your view of faith?

Understanding Luther's teaching means understanding his view of his own sin. The Bible teaches that we've all sinned and fall short of God's glory (see Rom. 3:23). Faith can't depend on us. Instead, we must shift confidence from our sinful selves to the perfect person and work of Christ.

Why is it important that faith isn't simply a belief but an act of trust?

If salvation is by grace alone through faith alone, what role do works have in our Christian walk?

The Roman Catholic Church taught that even faith had strings attached, in the form of works. The Reformers taught that Christians should do good works but only as an outflow of Christ living in us and working through us by the Holy Spirit. In ourselves we have no hope, but in Christ we have assurance that we're saved.

In what ways can you point others to Christ by showing them that their works can't justify them before God?

Close in prayer, thanking God for giving us the ability to have faith.

Complete the following three personal-study sections before the next group session.

THE BIG IDEA

No one can come to me unless the Father who sent me draws him.
And I will raise him up on the last day.
JOHN 6:44

As we mentioned in week 1, justification by faith alone is perhaps the cornerstone of the Reformation. This *sola* is the exact point where the theological rubber meets the Reformation road. All the key truths for Luther and his followers rested on the idea that we can't contribute to our salvation. As Luther said, we can never forget the truth of the gospel:

> *Here I must take counsel of the Gospel, I must hearken to the Gospel,*
> *which teacheth me, not what I ought to do …, but what Jesus Christ*
> *the Son of God hath done for me: … that he suffered and died to*
> *deliver me from sin and death. The Gospel willeth me to receive*
> *this, and to believe it. And this is the truth of the Gospel. It is also the*
> *principal article of all Christian doctrine, wherein the knowledge of*
> *all godliness consisteth. Most necessary it is therefore, that we should*
> *know this article well, teach it unto others, and beat it into their*
> *heads continually.*[1]

The Roman Catholic Church, with its extrabiblical doctrines and practices, had sent the gospel into eclipse. It had forgotten the *alone* side of the equation. The Church was adding so many ingredients to the recipe that it no longer looked like the gospel.

The world continually beats into our heads the belief that we can justify ourselves. We can be a good person if we just become a better parent, a better friend, or a better neighbor. If we're just kind enough to others, the world tells us, surely God won't judge us. But that's not true. Without Christ, God will surely judge us. After all, even spiritually dead people can be good neighbors. But that doesn't save anyone. We need more. We need

Jesus' life, death, burial, and resurrection because He's the only way to salvation (see John 14:6). We continually need to be reminded that when God looks at His sinful people, He sees the perfect righteousness of His Son. That's the only hope we have.

Record three ways you've recently tried to justify yourself.

1.

2.

3.

Now record three ways the gospel overrides those justifications.

1.

2.

3.

If we know we're sinful and we know we need a Savior, then pride shouldn't exist in our hearts. It's hard to be prideful when we look up at the beaten, bloodied Jesus hanging from the cross. Faith, then, should bring humility.

THE HUMILITY OF FAITH

You might have noticed that this week's study already sounds similar to last week's study of grace alone. Luther taught that we're justified by grace alone through faith alone. In other words, it's only the sheer grace of God that allows us sinners and rebels to have faith. Faith and grace are always tied together. We're saved by grace when we put our faith in Jesus Christ, but it's the work of grace that makes that faith genuine and alive.

Notice the connection between the two ideas in Paul's teaching:

By grace you have been saved through faith. And this is not your own
doing; it is the gift of God, not a result of works, so that no one may boast.
EPHESIANS 2:8-9

Salvation is God's gift to us, so both faith and grace are gifts. If God wanted to deny us faith or even the ability to have faith, He could. But because of His fierce love for us, He graciously provides a way for us to be saved through faith in His Son. We were dead in our sins, but by grace through faith, we're made alive in Christ (see Eph. 2:1-7).

How does it affect your walk with God to know that faith is a gift rather than something you've mustered?

In what ways do you act prideful instead of humble about the forgiveness Christ has given you?

In Ephesians 2:8-9 Paul made it clear: we're justified not by works but by grace through faith. The Roman Catholic Church was teaching contrary to this, but Paul is right. If we can contribute to our salvation, then we can boast. We might say, "God and I worked together on this. We make a great team!" But you and God aren't a team. Rather, God is the player, and you're the ball; you contribute only to the extent that He uses you. No one gives the ball credit for scoring a goal, nor should they.

Be encouraged by these powerful words:

Once you were not a people, but now you are God's people; once
you had not received mercy, but now you have received mercy.
1 PETER 2:10

THE EXPECTATION OF IMPUTATION

A core belief in the Reformation's teaching on justification is the idea that Christ imputed His righteousness to us. In other words, His righteousness is attributed or ascribed to us. His righteousness becomes our righteousness, so that our sinfulness is no longer the criterion by which God judges us. When God looks at us, He sees Jesus' righteousness instead of our sin.

This truth is why it's so dangerous to trust ourselves or anyone else for justification. As the writer of the Book of Hebrews tells us about Christ's sacrifice on the cross:

> *Nor was it to offer himself repeatedly, as the high priest enters the holy places every year with blood not his own, for then he would have had to suffer repeatedly since the foundation of the world. But as it is, he has appeared once for all at the end of the ages to put away sin by the sacrifice of himself.*
> **HEBREWS 9:25-26**

Every year the high priest in Israel entered the tabernacle and killed an animal, whose blood covered the sins of the people. Every year. Another animal. Another pool of blood. This practice was observed nonstop, year in and year out, for the people of Israel.

However, the writer of Hebrews gives us good news: Christ doesn't have to climb back up on the cross every year. He's the High Priest who made the sacrifice and was the sacrifice. He shed his blood once, for all of us. He did what no one else, not even the high priest of Israel, could do; He made the perfect, once-for-all sacrifice for sins (see Heb. 10:10).

Because the Jewish priest was never perfect, he wasn't qualified to sacrifice himself for our sin, and no single animal could fully satisfy God's wrath and justice toward sin. However, as a sinless Man and a spotless Lamb, Jesus Christ was able to make the perfect sacrifice for sin (see 1 Pet. 1:18-19). None of us can be Jesus, and God doesn't expect us to be. We should only expect Christ's righteousness to be imputed to us, by grace alone through faith alone. As Luther taught, righteousness isn't something we have; it's a gift we receive.[2]

Why are we unable to be righteous on our own?

THE WEIGHT OF SIN AND THE PEACE OF CHRIST

> *If anyone would feel the greatness of sin he would not be able*
> *to go on living another moment; so great is the power of sin.*[3]
> **MARTIN LUTHER**

Luther wasn't saying sin is great, as in really good. Rather, he was saying it's huge; it weighs on us like a million-ton stone made of guilt, shame, and frustration. Sometimes sin starts small with a simple desire that feels harmless. But sin doesn't play games. As James explained:

> *Desire when it has conceived gives birth to sin,*
> *and sin when it is fully grown brings forth death.*
> **JAMES 1:15**

According to James, sin is like a little baby who seems sweet and innocent at first but grows up to be a deadly monster. Sin brings death (see Rom. 6:23). This is what Luther meant when he said we couldn't live another moment if we realized our sin. Sin kills us—literally—and understanding that fact makes the gravity of our sin clearer.

Before reading the past few paragraphs, how would you have described sin?

After this brief introduction to salvation by faith alone, how would you change your past definition of *sin*?

The Bible teaches us that sin brings death and that we can't save ourselves by our own works. Because that's true, it's easy to see why faith alone is important. If you don't understand salvation by grace alone through faith alone, you'll keep trying to save yourself—and you'll fail. Your own attempts at salvation don't lead to eternal life but to eternal death. Luther saw the Roman Catholic Church sending people on a path to hell by telling them they could earn, buy, and sacrifice their way to heaven.

Luther and the Reformers taught a concept called *simul iustus et peccator,* which means "justified and at the same time sinners." We're saved, but we're not perfect. Luther later added the word *semper* ("always"): "always justified and at the same time always sinners." We don't become gradually justified; we're justified immediately and forever, even in our continually sinful state.[4] Thomas Schreiner explains it well:

> *Faith doesn't transport us to paradise immediately because we still struggle with sin. … Nevertheless, we also enjoy assurance because our righteousness isn't our own.*[5]

In the next section we'll take a look at what the idea of faith alone means for our daily lives. It's easy to say we're saved by grace alone through faith alone, but it's not as easy to believe it. Yet the good news of the gospel is that regardless of what we think or how we feel, we're justified by Christ's righteousness through faith. Sin weighs us down, but Christ lifts it off our shoulders and gives us peace.

Spend the next few moments praying that God will show you ways you're not believing that faith alone is enough. Acknowledge that you can't be your own savior. Only Jesus can save, by grace through faith.

1. Martin Luther, *A Commentary on Saint Paul's Epistle to the Galatians* (London: James Duncan, 1830), 75.
2. Thomas Schreiner, *Faith Alone: The Doctrine of Justification,* The Five Solas Series, ed. Matthew Barrett (Grand Rapids, MI: Zondervan, 2015), 43.
3. Martin Luther, as quoted in Timothy George, *Theology of the Reformers,* rev. ed. (Nashville: Broadman & Holman Publishing Group, 2013), 69.
4. Michael Reeves and Tim Chester, *Why the Reformation Still Matters* (Wheaton, IL: Crossway, 2016), 31.
5. Schreiner, *Faith Alone,* 46.

DIGGING DEEPER

> *If you have a true faith that Christ is your Saviour, then at once you have a gracious God, for faith leads you in and opens up God's heart and will, that you should see pure grace and overflowing love.*[1]
> **MARTIN LUTHER**

Becoming a Christian later in life gives you an interesting perspective on morality. Before Christ I didn't think a whole lot about morals. I didn't necessarily pursue any virtues because of something bigger than myself. More often I just tried to be a good kid so that I wouldn't get in trouble. I was nice, unselfish, and generally easy to get along with because these qualities benefited me. And when things didn't go my way, I often blamed other people. After all, I had tried my best to keep people happy; if they were upset, it was clearly their fault!

As we've discussed, it's easy to justify our own sins. It's easy to think we're good people and find ways to make ourselves look blameless. But Scripture says none of us are blameless. Our eyes always look outward for ways to justify ourselves, but we haven't trained our minds and hearts to look upward. Because of this spiritual blindness, sinful people can't see that they aren't capable of justifying themselves or anyone else. Justification comes from God alone because He alone is perfect.

Why is self-justification a burden?

How does having Christ's righteousness imputed to you offer you peace from self-justification?

FAITH AND WORKS

If our works can't justify us, we're left asking a pretty simple question: Why does anything we do matter? Isn't it true that our sins are washed away by grace through faith? Hasn't the whole point of this study been that works mean nothing to God? Well, not quite.

To be fair, these questions confused Luther too. He knew for sure that justification by faith alone was biblical and true, but he was perplexed by passages like this in the Book of James:

> *What good is it, my brothers, if someone says he has faith but does not have works? Can that faith save him? If a brother or sister is poorly clothed and lacking in daily food, and one of you says to them, "Go in peace, be warmed and filled," without giving them the things needed for the body, what good is that? So also faith by itself, if it does not have works, is dead. But someone will say, "You have faith and I have works." Show me your faith apart from your works, and I will show you my faith by my works. You believe that God is one; you do well. Even the demons believe—and shudder! Do you want to be shown, you foolish person, that faith apart from works is useless? For as the body apart from the spirit is dead, so also faith apart from works is dead.*
> **JAMES 2:14-20,26**

In a way, the Book of James drove Luther crazy. He notoriously called it an "epistle of straw" because it didn't seem to mesh well with Paul's writings on faith and grace. He thought it talked too much about works. It's worth noting, though, that Luther ultimately appreciated the power of its truth.[2] On the one hand, he offered (perhaps half-jokingly) to award anyone "who could reconcile James and Paul"; on the other hand, he himself found reconciliation between them:

> *Faith … is a living, restless thing. It cannot be inoperative. We are not saved by works; but if there be no works, there must be something amiss with faith.*[3]

James said, "Even the demons believe" (v. 19). How is true belief different from theirs?

Why are works necessary expressions of faith?

Luther and James both agreed: faith without works is dead. There's no such thing as faith that people can't see. The gospel is so powerful that it changes us and so wonderful that we can't contain it.

THAT GRACE MAY ABOUND

Paul asked (and then answered) an interesting question in his letter to the Romans:

> *Are we to continue in sin that grace may abound? By no means!*
> *How can we who died to sin still live in it?*
> **ROMANS 6:1-2**

It's a good question, isn't it? We're saved by grace through faith—no works required. Anytime people are given grace, they often exploit it. Grace causes us to rejoice in being free from the weight of sin, but it also makes us wonder what is and isn't permissible within the bounds of that grace.

As Paul said, sinning to receive more grace isn't within the realm of possibility. We're not set free from sin so that we can sin more; we're set free from sin so that we can appreciate the joy of not falling prey to it. Sin is a cruel slave master, and slaves don't want to go back to their abusive master. That's not freedom. True freedom is living the way God calls you to, not the way you want to.

Luther was right: faith without works is a sign of malfunction. Faith is a gift from God, and God doesn't give us dead, powerless gifts. Faith actually does something. It's alive, powerful, and transformative. By the power of the Holy Spirit, we're being conformed to the image of Christ (see Rom. 8:29; 2 Cor. 3:18). If we have faith, but our lives aren't on a path toward Christlikeness, something is wrong.

How often do you give in to temptation because you know you'll be forgiven?

On the other hand, how often do you rely on your own works apart from faith in Christ?

Luther affirmed that works don't justify us, but works show that we're justified. Before we place faith in Christ, our works are misplaced. Even our best efforts at being good people aren't aimed at being more like Christ. And there's nowhere deep down inside us to pull out perfection or holiness that matches Christ's. We may find good intentions and hard work, but we don't find Christlikeness. We don't have a shot at being more like Christ unless He gives us His righteousness.

In the end we shouldn't place faith in Christ merely to get enough grace to cover our sins, although His forgiveness is a wonderful thing. Instead, we should seek grace through faith so that we can be more like Christ. Humanity's purpose isn't just to be forgiven so that we can get to heaven someday; it's primarily to be like Christ. God justifies us through Christ's work, not ours, so Christ is the standard. When we become like Him, we're who we were made to be. And we become like Him by faith alone.

JUSTIFIED TOWARD HOPE

Since we have been justified by faith, we have peace with God through our Lord Jesus Christ. Through him we have also obtained access by faith into this grace in which we stand, and we rejoice in hope of the glory of God. Not only that, but we rejoice in our sufferings, knowing that suffering produces endurance, and endurance produces character, and character produces hope, and hope does not put us to shame, because God's love has been poured into our hearts through the Holy Spirit who has been given to us.
ROMANS 5:1-5

By faith alone we're declared righteous by God, the righteous Judge. We're condemned to eternal, tormenting prison because of sin, but Christ's righteousness pardons us from that punishment. We have peace with God only through Christ.

In the previous passage Paul tells us that not only do we have peace with God through faith in Christ, but we also have a reason to rejoice and have hope. This passage reinforces the point that faith in Christ is not only about the forgiveness of sins but also about what faith actually does in our lives. Faith brings forgiveness, forgiveness brings peace, peace brings hope, and hope brings endurance in suffering.

John Calvin argued that we must continually be reminded of our justification:

We would certainly find ourselves in a miserable condition if we had to again be afraid all of the time that God's grace could all of a sudden not be there for us anymore![4]

Calvin was right. How can we hope in God's promises if we're always terrified that He won't keep them? If God says He will save us, we must trust Him because His promises are true. No relationship can thrive if trust doesn't exist.

How often do you have a hard time believing God's promises?

Why can we trust all of God's promises?

In high school I had a girlfriend who broke up with me every time she saw me talking to another girl, only to ask me to date her again once she had cooled off. It was an endless cycle of immaturity and mistrust. Needless to say, I didn't end up marrying that girl.

Sometimes we treat God like a high-school boyfriend or girlfriend. When we're in a good mood or feel trusting, we give Him attention and admiration. But when we want our own way, when we're feeling selfish and insecure, we push Him away as though He's out to break our hearts. We accuse Him of holding out on us or ignoring us.

But God isn't like a high-school crush. He isn't fickle. His love doesn't flinch. Since we're justified by faith alone in Christ's perfect works, we can endure anything from a bad day to a Roman cross. Faith isn't blind; it sees clearly. And when its sights are set on the goodness of God, there's no room for fear, doubt, or worry.

Spend the next few moments praising God that He alone has saved you. Acknowledge that faith is a gift of grace you didn't earn and don't deserve.

1. Martin Luther, as quoted in Ronald H. Bainton, *Here I Stand: A Life of Martin Luther* (Nashville: Abingdon, 1978), 51.
2. Martin Luther, *Word and Sacrament I,* vol. 35 in *Luther's Works,* ed. E. Theodore Bachmann (Philadelphia: Fortress, 1960), 362, 395–97.
3. Martin Luther, as quoted in *Here I Stand,* 342.
4. John Calvin, as quoted in Michael Horton, *Calvin on the Christian Life: Glorifying and Enjoying God Forever* (Wheaton, IL: Crossway, 2014), 97.

GOSPEL APPLICATION

It is taught that good works should and must be done, not that a person relies on them to earn grace, but for God's sake and to God's praise. Faith alone always takes hold of grace and forgiveness of sin. Because the Holy Spirit is given through faith, the heart is also moved to do good works.[1]

PHILIP MELANCHTHON

This week we've discussed at length the truth that we're justified by God by grace through faith. Christ's righteousness pervades our sinful souls like an antibiotic in a sick person's bloodstream. We don't fight for healing; healing is given to us. The medicine of God's grace does the work.

But now we should ask a final question: How does our justification affect other people? It's great that we're Christians who have been transformed by the good news of the gospel and empowered by the Holy Spirit. We should praise God for the gift of faith. And yet we can't forget that faith doesn't terminate with us. Like grace, it's a gift that's meant to be shared.

How does the fact that faith is a gift from God change the way we view the opportunity for other people to come to faith?

The Roman Catholic Church said for people to know God, they had to come to the regular Church services and partake of the sacraments: baptism, Eucharist/Lord's Supper, confirmation, penance, holy matrimony, anointing of the sick, and holy orders. In other words, the Church's evangelism tool was a series of spiritual deeds overseen by the priest. It was grace—but grace that needed some human effort. If you asked, "How can I be justified by God?" the Church's answer was "Get to work." If that's not bad news, I don't know what is.

FAITH WORKS

Faith isn't about works, but faith works. As Melanchthon said so well, faith causes our hearts to do good works. But these faith-driven, grace-empowered works aren't simply good deeds, like being kind, patient, or generous. Of course, those things are good, but there's more. When asked what the greatest commandment was, Jesus replied that it's twofold:

> *You shall love the Lord your God with all your heart and with all your soul and with all your mind. This is the great and first commandment. And a second is like it: You shall love your neighbor as yourself. On these two commandments depend all the Law and the Prophets.*
> **MATTHEW 22:37-40**

Have you ever wondered why loving God and others is tied together like that? There's a very simple reason, with tons of potential for action. After all, "if God so loved us, we also ought to love one another" (1 John 4:11). Why? "If we love one another, God abides in us and his love is perfected in us" (1 John 4:12). In other words, we show God's love to other people by living it out, and we live it out because God first loved us. His love changes our attitude toward others.

What's the difference between doing a good deed and loving people as Christ loves them?

Why is it important to understand this difference?

This is faith in action: love God and love others. These two can't be separated, because our love of others actually flows from our faith in God.

We can't look at others with love if we aren't looking up at God with love, having experienced the love He sent down to us in Jesus.

Everyone loves someone or something, and most of us aren't ashamed of it. If you've truly been changed by the gospel—justified by grace alone through faith alone—your love for God will grow over time too. The more your love for God grows, the more it changes your heart toward others. Luther said it well: "Christian righteousness consists in two things: faith in the heart and the imputation of God."[2] Faith alone. Christ's righteousness alone. Now that's good news!

WHOSE JUSTIFICATION IS IT?

> *"The word is near you, in your mouth and in your heart" (that is, the word of faith that we proclaim); because, if you confess with your mouth that Jesus is Lord and believe in your heart that God raised him from the dead, you will be saved. For with the heart one believes and is justified, and with the mouth one confesses and is saved. For the Scripture says, "Everyone who believes in him will not be put to shame." For there is no distinction between Jew and Greek; for the same Lord is Lord of all, bestowing his riches on all who call on him. For "everyone who calls on the name of the Lord will be saved."*
> **ROMANS 10:8-13**

As we've discussed this week, it's not difficult to justify our own sins. We're self-serving to a fault. But when it comes to loving and serving others, it gets a little messier. It's easier to hide inside our house to read and pray, but it's quite another thing to walk across the street and talk with a borderline stranger. It's not as easy to give money to a ministry or give away something we cherish to someone who has nothing. But part of loving God is loving the people He has created. The greatest commandment, remember, is to love God and love others.

There are myriad ways to love others, but love can't ultimately end with a smile or a donation. Love must ultimately end with showing people a greater love than yours: the love of Christ. The previous passage clearly tells us: anyone ("there is no distinction," v. 12) who believes in Christ can be saved. Believe and confess. No additives.

> **Sometimes we make faith complicated, as though it needs to be faith plus extra beliefs or works. How does Romans 10 make faith easy to understand?**

> **How does the simplicity of faith encourage us to share the gospel with others?**

The Roman Catholic Church told people to follow a multistep process to receive the forgiveness of sins. This included sorrow, confession, making restitution, and a pledge not to commit this sin again. If a person completed the tasks, God would forgive them.[3] But the Reformers understood that justification for even the "smallest" sin doesn't come from our own striving.

If we agree with the Reformers' convictions, we shouldn't tell people they need more than simple faith to be justified before God. They should confess their sins and repent—yes—but they should understand that repentance is an act of obedience, not salvation. Calvin, in strong disagreement with the Roman Catholic Church, put it this way:

> *Repentance is not the cause of forgiveness of sins. … We have taught that the sinner does not dwell upon his own compunction or tears, but fixes both eyes upon God's mercy alone. We have merely reminded him that Christ called those who "labor and are heavy-laden," when he was sent to publish the good news to the poor, to heal the broken-hearted, to proclaim release to the captives, to free the prisoners, to comfort the mourners.[4]*

In other words, don't tell people who are tired of working to work harder. This line of thinking is what caused Luther to nearly faint when he performed his first mass. Jesus didn't preach a message of labor but a message of rest. He didn't preach a message of slavery but a message of freedom. This is the same message we preach today: that sinners are justified by faith alone in the grace and righteousness of Christ alone. It's His justification, not our own.

ON EARTH AS IT IS IN HEAVEN

Because of our sin we don't deserve God's love. He didn't have to send His Son to die on the cross for us. But He did. Jesus died in our place to give us His righteousness.

So if your neighbor isn't the nicest person in the world or your spouse drives you crazy sometimes, it's easy to believe they don't deserve for you to be kind to them. You're tempted to justify yourself in not being kind instead of remembering the justification you've received from God. You think, *Why should I serve this person who isn't serving me?* Because of the gospel. The gospel is the good news that even though you didn't deserve kindness, forgiveness, and mercy, by faith you received it anyway. Because God loved you, you can love others.

For a Christian, inaction isn't an option. We're drawn into God's love and then sent out to show it to the world. No one on this planet is as equipped as we are to show God's love, because God Himself lives inside us through the Holy Spirit. No one can compete with that qualification. Jesus told His disciples that not even "the gates of hell" stand a chance against God's gospel-carrying people (see Matt. 16:18). Jesus prayed to His Father:

> *Your kingdom come,*
> *your will be done,*
>   *on earth as it is in heaven.*
> **MATTHEW 6:10**

Jesus was asking for God's perfect will to be done here on this sinful, broken planet. We've been given the good news in a bad-news world, and that should inspire us to join God's plan to redeem sinners.

When we love others, we show them God's love. When we forgive others, we show them God's forgiveness. When we're patient with others, we show them God's patience. When we tell others the truth, we show them God's truth. When we sacrifice for others, we show them Christ's sacrifice on the cross. There's always a connection between our faith in God and our actions toward other people. Our works are always a product of our faith in a perfect, just, and loving God. A life lived in light of justification by faith alone shows others the beautiful reality that they too can be justified by faith alone.

Identify three people who need to hear the free offer of salvation by grace alone through faith alone in Christ alone.

1.

2.

3.

Spend the next few moments thanking God that He has made it possible for you to be justified by faith alone. Ask Him to help you be a proclaimer of rest and freedom, not work and slavery.

1. Philip Melanchthon, as quoted in Timothy J. Wengert, *Reading the Bible with Martin Luther: An Introductory Guide* (Grand Rapids, MI: Baker Academic, 2013), 87.
2. Martin Luther, as quoted in Wengert, *Reading the Bible with Martin Luther,* 116.
3. Michael Horton, *Calvin on the Christian Life: Glorifying and Enjoying God Forever* (Wheaton, IL: Crossway, 2014), 127.
4. John Calvin, as quoted in Horton, *Calvin on the Christian Life,* 127.

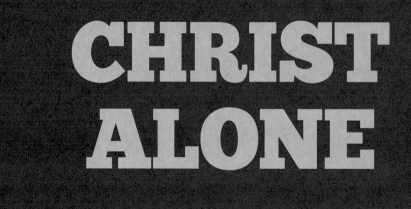

CHRIST ALONE

SESSION 5

START

Welcome to group session 5 of *Echoes of the Reformation*. Last week we explored the belief that faith alone justifies us. Answer these questions as you reflect on last week's study.

In what ways did the study of faith alone change the way you view your relationship with God?

How did learning more about faith alone affect your relationships with others?

When children learn colors, they learn how to tell blue from orange. When they learn shapes, they learn they can't fit a square peg in a round hole. All of us learn over time to live in the tension that some things are what they are and can't be changed. Day isn't the same as night, being happy isn't the same as being furious, and frozen yogurt definitely isn't ice cream.

Christianity is no different. Christians can't agree with culture's notion that many paths lead to God. Salvation through anyone but Christ might as well be frozen yogurt calling itself ice cream. Luther boldly preached this truth as he saw the Roman Catholic Church seating the pope and other leaders too close to Christ's throne:

> *Any true Christian, living or dead, possesses a God-given share in all the benefits of Christ and the church, even without indulgence letters.*[1]

To put it simply, through Christ alone Christians have all they need for salvation and every blessing that comes with it.

This week we'll see that Christ alone saves us. Watch video session 5 with your group.

WATCH

In Christ alone means all of Christ—everything taught about Christ in the entire Scriptures—and it means Christ and no one else.

It is to Christ alone that I must be faithful. I must be exclusively devoted to Jesus Christ above all else.

The New Testament model was that Christ is the answer to every question.

It's the object of the faith that saves us.

Your hope is not in how much faith you can muster up but in the greatness of the Savior.

Christianity alone explains what our problem is and why we need a Savior and how God in His mercy provided all that is necessary for us in Christ.

All that was necessary for our salvation was accomplished by Christ.

DISCUSS

On the video Albert Mohler, Kevin DeYoung, and Trevin Wax discussed the idea of *solus Christus*—Christ alone.

Why do you think this doctrine is still important today?

How did the video discussion challenge your view of Christ?

Christ alone—no one else—has accomplished our salvation. He's God in the flesh, who lived the life we can't live and died the death we deserve. And by rising from the dead, He defeated death to give us eternal life.

Why do we need to remember that faith is always directed at an object—Christ Himself?

Why can no person, apart from Christ, serve as a mediator between God and us?

The Roman Catholic Church taught that Christ alone was sufficient for salvation, but the church didn't really live out this doctrine in its teaching on works and the authority of the pope. Christians today struggle with the same inconsistency, saying we believe Christ alone can save but often relying on ourselves instead.

In what ways do you need to trust more in Christ and less in yourself?

Close in prayer, thanking God for salvation through Christ.

Complete the following three personal-study sections before the next group session.

---

1. Martin Luther, as quoted in Timothy J. Wengert, *Martin Luther's 95 Theses: With Introduction, Commentary, and Study Guide* (Minneapolis: Fortress, 2015), 18–19.

THE BIG IDEA

The summary of the gospel is that our Lord Christ, true Son of God, has made known to us the will of his Heavenly Father and has redeemed us from death and reconciled us with God by his guiltlessness. Therefore, Christ is the only way to salvation of all who were, are now, or shall be.[1]
HULDRYCH ZWINGLI

When asked how a person can inherit eternal life, Jesus answered:

I am the way, and the truth, and the life. No one comes to the Father except through me. If you had known me, you would have known my Father also. From now on you do know him and have seen him.
JOHN 14:6-7

Jesus made a clear statement: the only way a person can come to the Father (in other words, be saved and have eternal life) is through Him. He didn't say, "I am one of many ways, one of many truths, and one of many lives." He also didn't say, "No one can come to the Father except through Me, unless you're a really good person." One truth, one way, and one life lead to salvation—Jesus Christ.

Notice these statements earlier in the Gospel of John:

In the beginning was the Word, and the Word was with God, and the Word was God. He was with God in the beginning. All things were created through him, and apart from him not one thing was created that has been created. In him was life, and that life was the light of men. No one has ever seen God. The one and only Son, who is himself God and is at the Father's side—he has revealed him.
JOHN 1:1-4,18, CSB

God so loved the world, that he gave his only Son, that whoever believes in him should not perish but have eternal life. For God did not send his Son into the world to condemn the world, but in order that the world might be saved through him.
JOHN 3:16-17

No one can come to me unless the Father who sent me draws him. And I will raise him up on the last day. It is written in the Prophets, "And they will all be taught by God." Everyone who has heard and learned from the Father comes to me—not that anyone has seen the Father except he who is from God; he has seen the Father. Truly, truly, I say to you, whoever believes has eternal life.
JOHN 6:44-47

Even though Jesus was pointing back to the Father as the One who sent Him, He's the only One the Father sent and the only One through whom we can go to the Father. It's through Christ alone that we can be saved.

Go back to the previous passages and circle every occurrence of the words *Father* and *Son*.

Record three ways the relationship between the Father and the Son affects us.

1.

2.

3.

When the Roman Catholic Church told people that buying indulgences and confessing sins to the priests contributed to salvation, they were putting other saviors next to the true Savior. Church practice of Luther's day wasn't about Scripture alone, grace alone, or faith alone—and it certainly wasn't about Christ alone, because all those things flow from Him.

GOD IN THE FLESH

When Jesus was born in a manger about two thousand years ago, he didn't just make an impact on everything that would follow. His birth uprooted history and turned it on its head. Things in the past now meant something different. He wasn't just a special child. He wasn't merely the heir to a great kingdom. Rather, as Matthew 1:23 tells us, he was "Immanuel (which means, God is with us)." Christ was—is—God with 10 fingers and 10 toes.

Knowing that Jesus is God in the flesh makes more sense of the passages we read from the Gospel of John. The Bible declares over and over again that only God can save. This verse, for example, gives us a summary:

> For God alone my soul waits in silence;
> from him comes my salvation.
> **PSALM 62:1**

If only God can save, then only Jesus can save us if He Himself is God. Those passages from John tell us plainly that He's God and that He brings God's salvation.

Luther and the Reformers couldn't escape the truth of Christ alone, because the Bible wouldn't let them. Looking for other gods for salvation instead of the God-man was full of problems. Because none of those false gods were sent by the Father, they couldn't lead people to the Father.

Why is it important that Jesus is God?

When you think of Jesus, do you more often think of Him as God in the flesh or as a nice, moral teacher?

Last week we discussed justification by faith alone, and we learned that Christ's righteousness is the only righteousness that God will accept. As God in the flesh, Jesus carries the perfection and holiness of God. As humankind in the flesh, we carry the imperfection and sin of Adam. However, Jesus didn't walk the earth as a hologram of God. He was a real man in flesh and bones.

THE SECOND ADAM

Before sin entered the world, humankind was perfect. Adam and Eve lived in perfect harmony with God and with each other. But as Paul tells us in the Book of Romans, Adam brought sin and death into the world. From the beginning of our lives, we all inherit a sinful nature from our first father, Adam. One sin brought death and destruction into the world. One sin was all it took to separate God from His people, because sin can't dwell in God's presence—not even one.

To bring us back to God, there had to be a man who could be a mediator—a go-between—who could bridge the gap between God and His people. As we've already seen earlier in this study, Israel's priests tried to fill the gap. Every year they killed an animal as a sacrifice. But they had to do this every year, and even then it was never enough. In Luther's time paying indulgences, performing religious activities, and trying to be a good person were just as useless. The Roman Catholic Church was still pointing to something even God's law wasn't designed to do.

But God had a plan to redeem us. John Calvin explained it this way:

> [God determined] that the Mediator should be God, and become man. Neither man nor angel, though pure, could have sufficed. The Son of God behooved to come down.[2]

Calvin made an interesting point: not even a sinless angel could step in and save us. We would need a perfect man who would be the necessary mediator and substitute, so God Himself had to do the saving. It couldn't be an ordinary man; it had to be God in the flesh. There would need to be a second Adam to reverse the curse of the first Adam:

> *If, because of one man's trespass, death reigned through that one man, much more will those who receive the abundance of grace and the free gift of righteousness reign in life through the one man Jesus Christ.*
> **ROMANS 5:17**

How do you and I relate to Adam?

Why is it important to affirm that Jesus is both God and man?

Only God could save us, and only God could step foot on earth's soil and not be eternally tainted by its brokenness. Those every-year sacrifices pointed to a man who would not only stand in the gap as a priest but would also shed His blood as the sacrifice. Jesus lived the perfect life that Adam (and the rest of us) couldn't live. The righteousness of Christ alone is therefore all we need for salvation.

THE RESURRECTED SAVIOR

Imagine for a second that Jesus died on the cross and then stayed dead; He never walked out of the tomb. Let's say that to this day, his bone dust is still in a grave somewhere in the Middle East. Would that matter? He died as a substitute for our sins, so isn't that enough? Here's the way the apostle Paul would answer that question:

If Christ has not been raised, your faith is futile and you are still in your sins. Then those also who have fallen asleep in Christ have perished. If in Christ we have hope in this life only, we are of all people most to be pitied. But in fact Christ has been raised from the dead, the firstfruits of those who have fallen asleep. For as by a man came death, by a man has come also the resurrection of the dead. For as in Adam all die, so also in Christ shall all be made alive.

1 CORINTHIANS 15:17-22

According to Paul, Jesus' death is only half of the story. Yes, he died for our sins. Praise God! But more than that, he rose from the dead. Adam brought death into the world, so somebody had to bring life back to the world. If Jesus had remained dead, He wouldn't have really solved the problem of death. He would be just another man in a six-foot hole.

But Jesus came back to life so that we could have eternal life rather than the eternal death we received from Adam. Humankind was never supposed to die. Genesis 3–Revelation 20 is a story of sin and death, but God wants us to live in a Genesis 1–2 and Revelation 21–22 world, where sin and death don't exist and people are right with God. In Christ alone we can live eternally with our Creator just the way we were made to.

Why is it important that Jesus not only died for our sins but also rose from the dead?

Spend the next few moments asking God to show you that you're not a savior, and neither is anyone or anything else. Ask Him to help you see that Christ alone can save you, as well as all the implications of that wonderful truth.

1. Huldrych Zwingli, as quoted in Timothy George, *Theology of the Reformers,* rev. ed. (Nashville: Broadman & Holman Publishing Group, 2013), 129.
2. John Calvin, *Institutes of the Christian Religion,* trans. Henry Beveridge (Peabody, MA: Hendrickson, 2008), 297.

DIGGING DEEPER

> *We are forgiven for Christ's sake, who alone*
> *is the mediator to reconcile the Father.*[1]
> **PHILIP MELANCHTHON**

The previous lesson showed that Christ alone can save us. No imitation saviors will suffice. Neither will gathering up indulgences or begging priests for special prayers. Let's reflect on this reality for a moment.

Why can't a priest pray a special prayer to save us?

Why can't we save ourselves?

Salvation by grace alone through faith alone in Christ alone isn't simply a ticket to heaven. It also matters for our everyday lives. It's important for us to remember that God didn't wave a magic wand and eradicate all our sins. Instead, God in the flesh lived a real, human life and died a real, human death. Jesus lived a life we couldn't, but that doesn't mean our lives are disconnected from His.

Humankind is united with Christ. The Roman Catholic Church taught that Christians could have union with Christ but that it changed based on our works, namely prayer and repentance.[2] The Reformers, however, taught something more radical. They said union with Christ is steady and unchanging because His righteousness unites us with Him. And because His righteousness doesn't change, neither does our union with Him.

CHRIST IN ME

> *I have been crucified with Christ. It is no longer I who live, but Christ who lives in me. And the life I now live in the flesh I live by faith in the Son of God, who loved me and gave himself for me.*
> **GALATIANS 2:20**

The Reformers sought to encourage Christians that we don't rest in our own works but in the works of Christ alone.[3] The Roman Catholic Church had a whole list of works to choose from, but the doctrine of Christ alone scratched them all out, replacing the whole list with one word: *Christ*. The Reformers pointed out that the Church confused union with communion. Michael Reeves and Tim Chester offer a helpful explanation of the difference:

> *Communion with Christ—meaning the actual enjoyment of Christ— is something that fluctuates in believers. Sometimes our hearts are full of hallelujahs; sometimes they are frosty and unfeeling toward him. … The Puritan Richard Sibbes … put it like this: "Union is the foundation of communion." In Reformation thought, union with Christ is a fixed and therefore stable thing, the solid foundation on which we can know lasting joy.*[4]

So first things first: our source of joy isn't our own efforts or circumstances but the unwavering person of Christ. Our joy is bundled up in the warm blanket of God's grace and mercy, shown to us through Christ. We're united with Christ, as Galatians 2:20 says, because He lives in us. But there's even more to our union with Christ. It's not simply that He lives in us, though He does, and it's not simply that we see God through the work of Christ. It's also that God sees us through the work of Christ.

Thus, it's important to understand that our union with Christ is directly tied to the Father. So when we say, "When God looks at us, He doesn't see our sin; instead, He sees Jesus' righteousness," we're talking about our union with Christ. When Paul told the Galatians, "I have been crucified with Christ," he was talking about his union with Christ. We're so united with Him that we might as well have been on the cross with Him.

Mark a point on the scale to indicate how often you feel that Christ lives within you.

Never   Rarely   Sometimes   All the time

In what ways does Galatians 2:20 change your outlook on the fact that Christ lives within you?

THE FATHER'S LOVE FOR HIS SON

Calvin was perhaps the most powerful promoter of the Reformation idea of union with Christ. And Calvin correctly saw our union with Christ as more than a mere Catholics-versus-Protestants dictionary debate. It was more than words and definitions; it was about real life. As Michael Horton has said:

> *For Calvin, the Christian life is a daily feeding upon these riches. We never move on from the gospel, but grow more deeply into its nourishing soil, thereby bearing the fruit of love and good works. The supreme gift in this union is Christ himself, but he brings his gifts with him.*[5]

Do you see that? We get the gift of Christ Himself, and we get everything that comes with it. Paul said to the Ephesians:

> *Blessed be the God and Father of our Lord Jesus Christ, who has blessed us in Christ with every spiritual blessing in the heavenly places.*
> **EPHESIANS 1:3**

What are these blessings? Paul went on to list several, using the phrase "in him"; we get all these things in or through our union with Christ:

- We were chosen before the foundation of the world (see v. 4).
- We're holy and blameless (see v. 4).
- We were predestined to be adopted as sons (see v. 5).
- We have grace lavished on us (see vv. 6,8).
- We have redemption and forgiveness through His blood (see v. 7).
- We know the mystery of God's will to redeem all things (see v. 9).
- We have an eternal inheritance of salvation (see v. 11).
- We have the ability to bring praise to God's glory (see v. 12).
- We heard the gospel (see v. 13).
- We were sealed by the Holy Spirit never to lose our salvation (see vv. 13-14).

Your next birthday or Christmas wish list might seem a little lame compared to this. This passage and many others tell us that because of our union with Christ, we're loved the way the Father loves His Son—eternally, unconditionally, and generously. God love us each individually, yes, but these gifts aren't about us; they're about Christ. His righteousness and His relationship with the Father are ours, not so that we can be puffed up with pride but so that we can fall to our knees in humble worship. The Father has perfectly loved the Son for eternity, and He loves us the same way.

> It's one thing to know something is true, but it's another thing to believe it. Circle the gifts in the previous list that are the hardest for you to believe.

> Stop and pray that God will help you believe the truth of these gifts that are yours in Christ Jesus.

UNION SPARKS COMMUNION

The Reformers saw something the Roman Catholic Church apparently missed: our salvation is anchored in Christ alone. He alone is our justifier. Because of His righteousness we're all justified even though we're sinners. Therefore, this union with Christ should lead to communion with Christ.

We saw the priceless gifts that come with being saved by grace through faith in Christ. These gifts don't just get dropped into our laps every so often, whenever God is having a good day. We receive all these gifts all the time, from the beginning (when we hear the gospel; see Eph. 1:13) to the end (when we're sealed by the Holy Spirit so that we never fall away from Him; see vv. 13-14).

How does the Holy Spirit's work affect our union with Christ?

The Holy Spirit is God. How does that truth affect your reading of Ephesians 1:13-14?

We have everything we need in Christ alone. Through Him we're saved by grace through faith. His life is now our life; His righteousness is now our righteousness; His gifts from the Father are now our gifts. The only offering we can lay before Him is the sin that nailed Him to the cross. But because He's righteous, holy, and good, He went to the cross with joy in order to unite us with Himself (see Heb. 12:1-2).

This love that unites us should carry us into full communion with Christ. His love is so mighty that it can and should overcome our tendency to disobey and ignore Him.

A TRUE UNION

Scripture uses the metaphor of marriage to describe our union and communion with Christ. I'm committed to my wife because I promised on our wedding day that my love for her would reflect Christ's love for me. So I'm all in, no matter what. My love for her doesn't depend on which side of the bed she wakes up on. When either of us has a bad day, we don't start talking about divorce. My wife has said many times that her favorite thing about me isn't my looks or personality (not surprising!) but my consistent love for her regardless of the circumstances. I say the same about her. Our union strengthens our communion.

As Paul said in Ephesians 5, my union with my wife is a small window into my union with Christ. God's love for us isn't dependent on what kind of day we have, and His commitment to us is stronger than any human marriage vow. We're united to Him forever, and He will never walk out on us.

Let's conclude this lesson with a powerful quotation by Luther:

> *Christ is full of grace, life, and salvation. The soul is full of sins, death, and damnation. Now let faith come between them and sins, death, and damnation will be Christ's, while grace, life, and salvation will be the soul's; for if Christ is a bridegroom, he must take it upon himself the things which are his bride's and bestow upon her the things that are his. … Who then can fully appreciate what this royal marriage means? Who can understand the riches of the glory of this grace? Here this rich and a divine bridegroom Christ marries this poor, wicked harlot, redeems her from all her evil, and adorns her with all his goodness. Her sins cannot now destroy her, since they are laid upon Christ and swallowed up by him. And she has that righteousness in Christ, her husband, of which she may boast as of her own and which she can confidently display alongside her sins in the face of death and hell and say, "If I have sinned, yet my Christ, in whom I believe, has not sinned, and all his is mine and all mine is his."*[6]

Spend the next few moments asking God to help you see that it's through Christ that you're loved. You have nothing apart from Christ alone. Praise God now for all He gives you through Christ.

1. Philip Melanchthon, as quoted in Timothy J. Wengert, *Reading the Bible with Martin Luther: An Introductory Guide* (Grand Rapids. MI: Baker Academic, 2013), 86.
2. Michael Reeves and Tim Chester, *Why the Reformation Still Matters* (Wheaton, IL: Crossway, 2016), 116–17.
3. Ibid., 117.
4. Ibid..
5. Michael Horton, *Calvin on the Christian Life: Glorifying and Enjoying God Forever* (Wheaton, IL: Crossway, 2014), 94.
6. Martin Luther, *Martin Luther: Selections from His Writings,* ed. John Dillenberger (New York: Anchor, 1962), 60–61.

GOSPEL APPLICATION

Faith must be taught correctly, namely, that by it you are so cemented to Christ that He and you are as one person, which cannot be separated but remains attached to Him forever.[1]
MARTIN LUTHER

You might get a hundred different answers if you asked random people on the street, "Who is Jesus?" You'd be hard-pressed in America to find someone who didn't at least know His name. It would be difficult, however, to find people who could truly articulate how the Bible describes Him. Jesus might be the most misunderstood and doubted man of all time. Some people call Him merely a good teacher, while others say He's a made-up character in a fictional book.

But if Jesus really was who said He was, our only response is worship. The question before us is whether we'll go and tell the world who He really is. In the quotation we read, Luther nailed it: "Faith must be taught correctly," and union with Christ is the cornerstone truth of our faith. The gospel rests on the belief that God is redeeming all things through Christ, and therefore salvation can't come to anyone who isn't first united to Him. Only the Redeemer can redeem.

How do union and communion with Christ affect the way we view those around us?

In this last section of study, we'll learn more about faith "taught correctly."

THE GOOD DEPOSIT

Follow the pattern of the sound words that you have heard from me, in the faith and love that are in Christ Jesus. By the Holy Spirit who dwells within us, guard the good deposit entrusted to you.
2 TIMOTHY 1:13-14

Writing to his apprentice, the young pastor Timothy, Paul gave a very clear command to protect the teaching that was passed down from Paul. This teaching, of course, is the gospel: "the faith and love that are in Christ Jesus" (v. 13). Paul wanted to make sure Timothy wasn't adding to or taking away from the gospel, "for it is the power of God for salvation to everyone who believes" (Rom. 1:16). A false gospel saves no one; only the true gospel has power.

One of our most beloved hymns says, "In Christ alone my hope is found."[2] We're called to bring this good news to a bad-news world, telling it that Jesus is more than a good teacher. If we're truly guarding the good deposit and correctly teaching it to others, then we're primarily telling them about the hope found in uniting with Christ by grace through faith.

Being united with Christ means who He is changes who we are. In Him our life's goal isn't to be nicer or happier; it's to become more and more like Him. God's Son stepped out of perfect eternity into our mess to proclaim the truth about Himself. He didn't come to earth on the greatest mission trip of all time so that we could sit back and get lazy after we've said a magical prayer. Instead, He came to gather a hell-shattering, God-worshiping task force to change the world forever (see Matt. 16:18). He's the embodiment of gospel truth; being like Him means guarding the good deposit and correctly teaching the faith to others.

Record three false gospels the world teaches today.

1.

2.

3.

Now record ways the true gospel supplants each false gospel.

1.

2.

3.

WHY WE AVOID SHARING THE GOSPEL

There are myriad reasons we don't share the gospel. For some of us, it's a matter of being too busy to think about it. For others, it's more about a fear of looking silly or being disliked. Whatever the excuse, we ultimately don't share the gospel because we forget the beauty of being united with Christ. As Reeves and Chester put it:

> The reason we are able to forget our union with Christ is that we have yet to experience the full glory of what it will mean. For now, we are members of Christ's body, but we still wander, our bodies still ache, and we shall still die.[3]

In other words, we don't always grasp the full meaning of what eternity will look like. This failure causes us to forget our union with Christ. When the sting of cancer is in our bones, it's hard to remember that one day pain will be no more. We're living in the already and the not yet; we're already redeemed, but we're not yet living in perfect eternity. We won't fully experience that until Christ returns. Until then it's a battle to look at eternity down the road when sin and death are in our passenger seat.

We don't share the gospel with others because we don't feel the weight of what it would mean not to be united with Christ. A person who spends eternity apart from God will receive none of the blessings we saw in Ephesians 1. No inheritance. No abounding grace. No eternal security in the Holy Spirit. That list of gifts we receive through Christ is the greatest news any person anywhere could receive. When we forget that we get Christ and everything else with Him, we don't feel the urgency to share the good news about that gift with others.

What struggles in your life cause you lose sight of eternity?

What does the doctrine of Christ alone say about an eternal perspective?

ALL AUTHORITY

Jesus came and said to them, "All authority in heaven and on earth has been given to me. Go therefore and make disciples of all nations, baptizing them in the name of the Father and of the Son and of the Holy Spirit, teaching them to observe all that I have commanded you. And behold, I am with you always, to the end of the age."
MATTHEW 28:18-20

I'm most afraid to share the gospel when I think I have to be the authority on the gospel. When I talk to my neighbor Neil, I often pull away from talking about the gospel right when I know I need to. Why? Because I'm afraid that I'll say something wrong or that I'll be a barrier to the gospel rather than an open door. Even though I have three degrees in theology, I'm still insecure about not knowing enough to talk to others about Jesus.

But believing that Christ alone saves people is actually more potent than any degree. The problem is that sometimes I would rather rely on all the books I've read rather than the Book I wish I read more often. If we're putting the authority to save people on ourselves, we're heading into a suicide mission in which everyone jumps on our shoulders, but we get crushed under their weight. As the previous passage states, Jesus Christ has the authority, not us. We all have excuses for not sharing the good news, and that's mine. But I'm guessing you can relate.

Why aren't we authorities on the gospel?

In what ways does the doctrine of Christ alone make evangelism less frightening?

Matthew 28 is the last chapter in Matthew's Gospel, and these are Jesus' last words to His disciples before He went back to heaven. The last thing someone says to you is often the most important. So when Jesus was sending out His disciples for the last time, He didn't just tell them to go; He told them to go in His authority.

It's strange that I've read or heard this passage countless times, and I always forget the first line. I skip right to the verbs *go, make, baptize, teach,* and even *behold,* but verbs without a subject are aimless. Why am I going? Whose disciples am I making and baptizing? What am I teaching? Who or what am I beholding?

The Roman Catholic Church ran into this verb-without-a-subject problem too. The Church constantly talked about works but didn't focus on the foundation of those works. Luther and the Reformers rightly remind us that because we're united with Christ, we do everything through and because of Him.

LIKE GOD BUT NOT GOD

If you read enough of Luther's teachings, you might think he was brash and even arrogant. At times he surely was, as we all are. But there was something more behind the man who ignited the Reformation. In trying to reform the Church, Luther didn't want to make it about him, and he used shocking language to make this point:

> *The first thing I ask is that people should not make use of my name, and should not call themselves Lutherans but Christians. What is Luther? The teaching is not mine. Nor was I crucified for anyone. … How did I, poor stinking bag of maggots that I am, come to the point where people call the children of Christ by my evil name?*[4]

Maybe it's a little strong to call oneself a "bag of maggots." Humankind is made in God's image and by faith is united with Christ. Humans have value far beyond anything in creation because of that fact. But we should also understand that Christ alone can save. Luther was right: none of us were crucified for the sins of the world. We're made in God's image, but we aren't God. We reflect Him; we don't replace Him.

Our world is looking for saviors everywhere, and it doesn't need us to pretend we're the savior they're looking for. Instead, we should tell them the good news that by grace through faith, they can be justified by God and united with Christ. In this simple act of obedience, we properly attribute authority to Christ, and we merely guard the good deposit delivered to us.

In what ways can you reflect Christ to those around you?

Why is it important not only to reflect Christ but also to guard the good deposit?

Name three people in your life who need to hear the good news of Christ alone.

1.

2.

3.

Spend the next few moments asking God to make you aware of the beauty of being united with Christ. Ask Him to let that realization spark a fire in you to tell others about Christ.

1. Martin Luther, as quoted in Michael Reeves and Tim Chester, *Why the Reformation Still Matters* (Wheaton, IL: Crossway, 2016), 122.
2. Keith Getty and Stuart Townend, "In Christ Alone," in *Baptist Hymnal* (Nashville: LifeWay Worship, 2008), 506.
3. Reeves and Chester, *Why the Reformation Still Matters*, 127.
4. Martin Luther, as quoted in Timothy George, *Theology of the Reformers*, rev. ed. (Nashville: Broadman & Holman Publishing Group, 2013), 54.

GLORY TO GOD ALONE

SESSION 6

START

Welcome to group session 6 of *Echoes of the Reformation*. Last week we explored the truth that Christ alone saves us. Answer these questions as you reflect on last week's study.

Name one savior you've elevated above the true Savior.

How can you put that savior aside and focus on Christ alone?

Have you ever seen a movie that starts at the end? It sounds crazy at first, doesn't it? But sometimes starting at the end makes the rest of the movie more meaningful. When you know the end of the story, you know how a character's decision will affect his or her life. It makes you say, "No! If you do that, you're in trouble!" Or it makes a particular scene even more epic. It also helps you see how the storyteller is putting all the details together.

In the same way, God reveals the end to us. If we read Revelation 22, we see the final act of a story that lasts for eternity. This story was written to motivate us to worship the Storyteller, to see His glory from start to finish. In the words of John Calvin, the world is God's "theater."[1]

This week we'll see that God's glory affects all the other *solas*. Watch video session 6 with your group.

WATCH

The end of all the *why* questions is God and His glory.

HOW GOD'S GLORY IS REVEALED IN SCRIPTURE

1. God's intrinsic reality
2. The external manifestation of God's glory

Luther didn't believe in a theology that brought glory to the sinner or to the church. It was a theology that brought glory to God alone, pointing to His saving work on the cross.

You're not the center of all things. You don't have to be the center of all things. And you'll never have the joy that you can have in Christ until you realize that that burden is not meant to be yours.

God's glory assures me that I will be saved and eternally that I am safe and secure in this self-glorifying God's promises and power.

Wisdom comes by knowing God and His glory, and then you understand your own fallenness and humility in how far from that you are.

God alone is worthy of glory.

Our greatest joy is going to be to glorify God forever.

DISCUSS

On the video Albert Mohler, Kevin DeYoung, and Trevin Wax discussed the idea of *soli Deo gloria*—glory to God alone.

Why do you think this doctrine is still important today?

How did the video discussion challenge your view of God's glory?

God's glory is the end of all the *why* questions of life. His glory is the sum total of who He is and what He does. God is the final answer to all our deepest longings. Because He's perfect and holy, He alone is glorious and deserves to be glorified.

How does God's glory affect our daily lives?

Why is it important for salvation to be directly connected to God's glory?

The Roman Catholic Church, by denying the *alone* aspect of all these doctrines, ultimately took glory away from God. People could steal a little glory for themselves by doing a good work or by performing a duty pre-scribed by the Church. But the Reformers were clear because Scripture is clear: only God receives the glory.

In what ways do you try to steal glory from God?

Close in prayer, thanking God for revealing His glory to us.

Complete the following three personal-study sections to conclude this Bible study.

---

1. John Calvin, *Institutes of the Christian Religion*, trans. Henry Beveridge (Peabody, MA: Hendrickson, 2008), 27.

THE BIG IDEA

The Bible says the whole earth is filled with God's glory:

> *Blessed be the LORD, the God of Israel,*
> *who alone does wondrous things.*
> *Blessed be his glorious name forever;*
> *may the whole earth be filled with his glory!*
> *Amen and Amen!*
> **PSALM 72:18-19**

What does it mean for the earthy to be filled with God's glory? What is God's glory?

In short, God's glory is the sum total of who He is and what He does. It's a powerful force that exudes from His entire being. He's eternal. He's perfect. He's good. He's loving. He's beautiful. He's just. He's sovereign over all things. We clearly see God's glory in creation, which shows that He's sovereign, all-powerful, and beautiful, and we clearly see God's glory in salvation, which shows that He's loving, just, and merciful.

Luther saw trouble in the Roman Catholic Church because its works-based offer of salvation was stealing glory from God. Because the Church acted as a filter between people and God, some of His glory was being overshadowed. More than that, the Church's system was giving people room to boast in their good works and achievements. As David VanDrunen points out, the Reformers saw that the Bible tells another story:

> *Simply put, the fact that salvation is by faith alone, grace alone,*
> *and Christ alone, without any meritorious contribution on our part,*
> *ensures that all glory is God's and not our own. Likewise, the fact*
> *that Scripture alone is our final authority ... protects the glory*
> *of God against every human conceit.*[1]

Because no one else is God, no one else can share His glory. As we've emphasized before, we're not God. He doesn't share His glory (see Isa. 48:11). And being prideful about our own efforts and good deeds attempts to steal God's glory. As Psalm 72:18 says, "[God] alone does wondrous things." Furthermore, as we'll see, the humility of God Himself hanging on the cross erases any shred of pride we have left.

Read Psalm 72:18-19 again. Name some ways you see God's glory in everyday life.

Examine your life and name three ways you intentionally or unintentionally steal glory from God.

1.

2.

3.

GLORY AND HUMILITY IN THE CROSS

> *It is not sufficient for anyone, and it does him no good to recognize God in his glory and majesty, unless he recognizes him in the humility and shame of the cross.*[2]
> **MARTIN LUTHER**

For Luther and the Reformers, the question was simple: How can anyone recognize God's glory if they don't look at Christ? As Hebrews 1:3 tells us, "He is the radiance of the glory of God and the exact imprint of his nature." If you want to see God's glory, look into the face of Jesus.

But this immediately creates a dilemma, doesn't it? We said part of recognizing God's glory is seeing that He's eternal, perfect, and all-powerful.

But Jesus, God in the flesh, didn't seem all that powerful while hanging on the cross. What's glorious about the God of the universe bleeding to death one weekend in Rome? The point of the cross, however, is crucial. The cross wasn't an executioner's chair; it was a King's throne. It looked like death had won again. But Christ's death killed death. It unbroke all that was broken.

For Luther, however, to behold the glory of God meant to behold Him crucified on a cross. Just as Christ humbled Himself on the cross, we too must humble ourselves and see the glory of God in a beaten and battered Savior.[3] Pride says we can't worship or see glory in a God who would die, but humility acknowledges that His death brought life. Remember, He didn't stay dead; He walked out of His grave so that we could one day walk out of ours. Defeating death is quite glorious, isn't it?

Have you ever thought of Jesus' torture on the cross as glorious? Why or why not?

In what way was Jesus' humility glorious?

Luther's point was simple: the only way we know God's glory is through His showing it to us, and the primary way He has shown it to us is through salvation found in Christ. Again, God's glory is both who He is and what He does. And what He did was to step into human history and lay down His life for us.

JESUS: THE RADIANCE OF GOD'S GLORY

We've seen that on the cross Jesus showed God's glory in a rather unexpected way. But Jesus also reflected God's glory in His life and ministry.

Jesus was clear about His relationship with His Father throughout His ministry. For example, He often said things like "If you had known me, you would have known my Father also" (John 14:7) and "Whatever you ask in my name, this I will do, that the Father may be glorified in the Son." (v. 13). In other words, if you want to see God's glory, look into the face of Jesus.

Think about it. If God's glory is who He is and what He does and Jesus is God in the flesh, then of course we see God's glory when we see Jesus. God's glory is seen in Jesus' holiness, perfection, love, kindness, and so much more. Who was more holy, perfect, loving, kind, and so much more than Jesus Christ?

> *He is the radiance of the glory of God*
> *and the exact imprint of his nature.*
> **HEBREWS 1:3**

Jesus is the exact expression of God—an identical mirror. When you see Him, you see the Father and the glory of God. He's a walking, talking representation of God's glory.

Christians often wish they could see God in all His glory. We think it might strengthen our belief or help us worship him more meaningfully. But the Israelites showed that this isn't the case. They saw God's glory on Moses' face in Exodus 34:29-35 and yet still struggled with disobedience and doubt throughout their entire history.

We don't need special dreams or kids-who-went-to-heaven books to believe in the real, tangible glory of God. We don't need a video of Jesus healing people or walking out of the tomb. Instead, we need to open our Bibles and look at the words that talk about God, Jesus, and the Holy Spirit. Our Bibles contain God's words, and God's words are true; His glory is spread out all over the pages. Then look at the sky, and you'll see the handiwork of God that shouts his glory too. As Ray Ortlund has said, "Stare at the glory of God until you see it."[4] God's glory is there, and we can see it even when life is hard.

Which statement describes you more accurately?
☐ I see God's glory in the good moments in life.
☐ I see God's glory in suffering and frustration.

How can you strike a balance in giving God glory in both the good and the bad?

THE POWER OF GOD'S GLORY

In the Old Testament believers couldn't look directly at God's glory without being dramatically changed. When Moses came down the mountain after meeting with God, God's glory shone so bright from Moses' face that the Israelites couldn't even look at him (see Ex. 34:30). When the prophet Isaiah saw God, he trembled at His majesty (see Isa. 6:1-5).

In the New Testament people were able to see God's glory in the person of Jesus. Because He was truly God in a truly human body, people were able to hug God's glory rather than be ruined by it. Even in the amazing event called the transfiguration, in which the glory of God shone from Jesus, His disciples were able to see it clearly. After witnessing this event, as well as and Jesus' life, miracles, death, and resurrection, Peter was able to say, "We were eyewitnesses of his majesty" (2 Pet. 1:16).

Luther wanted people to be witnesses of God's glory for themselves, not through a tinted window constructed by the Roman Catholic Church's works-based system. The Church wasn't the keeper of God's glory, and the pope needed to avoid glorifying his office. God's glory can't be contained by anyone or anything—not even the pope and the Church.

When you stand next to a plane while its engines are running, not only do you know the engines are on, but you also feel them. The sheer power of what they are and what they do makes your chest vibrate. In an infinitely more powerful way, God's glory is a soul-vibrating, life-changing force. It's not just a description of who He is and what He does; it's the pulsing brilliance of His eternal identity. His glory rocks us to the core. And through Scripture and creation around us, we too are eyewitnesses of His majesty.

Although we haven't physically seen Christ with our eyes, in what ways can we say with Peter that we're "eyewitnesses of his majesty"?

Instead of pleading for God to reveal His glory to us as He did to Moses, Isaiah, or the disciples, let's take to heart what Jesus said about us to His disciples: "Have you believed because you have seen me? Blessed are those who have not seen and yet have believed" (John 20:29). God's glory is readily available to us right now through faith in Christ.

All the echoes of the Reformation find their sound in God's glory. Remember that Church in Luther's day didn't deny the importance of Scripture, grace, faith, and Christ in salvation. But if someone asked about "the little word *alone,* we would soon find genuine disagreement."[5]

God's glory is God's glory only if it's alone. It can't be shared or watered down. Salvation is by grace alone through faith alone in Christ alone, found on the pages of Scripture alone. God receives all the glory because he does it all; everything is from Him. Drink deeply from the well of this truth and stare at the glory of God until you see it.

Spend the next few moments asking God to help you believe His glory is real, powerful, and life-changing. Ask Him to help you see His glory in the pages of the Bible and in the beautiful world around you.

1. David VanDrunen, *God's Glory Alone: The Majestic Heart of Christian Faith and Life,* The Five Solas Series, ed. Matthew Barrett (Grand Rapids, MI: Zondervan, 2015), 16.
2. Martin Luther, as quoted in VanDrunen, *God's Glory Alone,* 13.
3. VanDrunen, *God's Glory Alone,* 13.
4. Ray Ortlund, as quoted in Jared C. Wilson, *The Wonder-Working God: Seeing the Glory of Jesus in His Miracles* (Wheaton, IL: Crossway, 2014), 108.
5. VanDrunen, *God's Glory Alone,* 14.

DIGGING DEEPER

> *I consider that the sufferings of this present time are not worth comparing with the glory that is to be revealed to us.*
> **ROMANS 8:18**

Bruce Springsteen's famous song "Glory Days" describes people who live in the past. It talks about the former star baseball player and the prettiest girl back in high school, sitting at the bar late at night wishing things were the way they used to be. They're thinking about the glory days.

At some point in time, we've probably all had glory days. Back when we were more popular, had more money, were in better shape, or saw our whole lives ahead of us. Back when people cared about our status. Back when we felt that we represented something greater than ourselves. Back when we felt confident about ourselves.

When life punches us in the mouth or just doesn't work out the way we wanted, it's easy to wish things were different. So sometimes we idealize the past, forgetting that in a sinful world nothing is ever perfect. We had troubles then too, but frustration is a great distorter of memory.

Yet God says the glory days are ahead of us, not behind us. The story He's telling looks to the past only to point us to the future. Yes, Genesis 3 happened, but Revelation 21–22 is coming. And it's God's glory alone that will bring our glorious future.

Mark a point on the scale to indicate how often you wish you were in a different time of life.

Never   Rarely   Sometimes   All the time

How does God's glory inform the way you look at the past?

CREATED TO GLORIFY GOD

> *He has made everything beautiful in its time. Also, he has put eternity into man's heart, yet so that he cannot find out what God has done from the beginning to the end. I perceived that there is nothing better for them than to be joyful and to do good as long as they live; also that everyone should eat and drink and take pleasure in all his toil—this is God's gift to man. I perceived that whatever God does endures forever; nothing can be added to it, nor anything taken from it. God has done it, so that people fear before him.*
> **ECCLESIASTES 3:11-14**

God "has put eternity into man's heart" (v. 11). In other words, whether or not you recognize it, you were created to worship Him. This design isn't because He's selfish or because He's lonely but because the most joyful thing you could ever do is to worship God. He's the source of the greatest joy in the universe, and He wants you to worship Him and live full of joy. To glorify God is to recognize and give Him due worship for who He is and what He does.

Read Ecclesiastes 3:11-14 again. Circle any words in the passage that refer to God, including pronouns.

In what ways does this passage give glory to God?

What do these statements about God's glory and the frequency of their occurrence in this passage suggest about our own lives?

Commercials and self-help gurus tell you to be true to yourself and to write your own story. But that doesn't work, and we know it. It's a lie that makes us feel trapped every time we believe it, because it always fails to deliver lasting happiness. Sin tells us we're going to find satisfaction, but it never truly lives up to its promises. We miss true joy when we live for our glory instead of God's.

As Paul told the Corinthians, everything we do is for God's glory (see 1 Cor. 10:31). Every little thing can glorify God, from enjoying a meal to doing missionary work in China. If our lives were created for God's glory, then nothing we do can be detached from it. Instead, what we do either glorifies Him or doesn't; there's no gray area. But by grace alone through faith alone in Christ alone, we're freed to give glory to God alone.

FREE TO WORSHIP

Because Jesus left heaven and came to earth, because He died on the cross and walked out of the grave, we've received great freedom. We're released from the power of sin and set free to live for God's glory.

Psalm 19:1 tells us, "The heavens declare the glory of God." This means everything around us is shouting through a megaphone that God is here, right now, in every little detail of our lives. He knows us and wants us to know Him. His glory is everywhere, compelling us to worship Him, pulling our hearts toward Him. When we recognize God's glory, when we become aware that He's been right there the whole time, there's nothing to do but worship Him. His glory shows us that through Jesus His love is bigger than our sin. He will forgive us every single time. We can lay our lives at His feet and say, "It's Yours. I'm Yours." He won't reject us. He wants to make us whole.

The Book of Revelation tells us that God will make all things new in the end. Everything that's broken will become unbroken. One day no one will be blind to His glory. Everyone will see it. God tells us in Revelation 22:5 that His glory will be so bright, so clear, that we won't need the sun anymore!

We can read the final scene in the Bible right now. And because we've already seen the end, we know things will work out for good. We know that our lives aren't wasted and that the story is about the glory of God, not about how many times we've fallen down.

The Westminster Catechism says we exist "to glorify God, and to enjoy him forever."[1] Right here and now, before that final scene comes, God wants more and more people to see His glory because that's why they were created. God saves us from sin and points us to the end so that we'll spend eternity with Him. Though the future is coming, we're free right now to clearly see His glory and to worship Him.

On the average week how often do you look forward with hope toward the future God has for you?

☐ Less than once

☐ Once

☐ More than once

How can you worship God now, even while living in a broken world?

FUTURE GLORY

The chief good of man is nothing else but union with God.[2]

JOHN CALVIN

Last week we discussed the Reformers' distinction between union with Christ and communion with Christ. Through our union with Christ, God sees us as He sees His Son—perfect and blameless. This union is rock-solid and unchanging. Our communion with Christ, however, can change, depending on our hearts. We don't always fully give our lives to Him as we should.

Our glory days that lie ahead will come only through our union with Christ. After all, we'll spend eternity with God in that glorious future only because of grace alone through faith alone in Christ alone. Our future is grounded in that union. But the way we glorify God is through our communion with Him. We can't worship Him in all His glory if we ignore His glory.

List three reasons you struggle in your communion with God.

1.

2.

3.

In what ways does your union with God help drive your communion with Him?

Will it always be this way? Will we always have a steady union but a shaky communion? The Bible seems to say no. Paul told the Corinthians:

> *Those whom he foreknew he also predestined to be conformed to the image of his Son, in order that he might be the firstborn among many brothers. And those whom he predestined he also called, and those whom he called he also justified, and those whom he justified he also glorified.*
> **ROMANS 8:29-30**

> *We all, with unveiled face, beholding the glory of the Lord, are being transformed into the same image from one degree of glory to another. For this comes from the Lord who is the Spirit.*
> **2 CORINTHIANS 3:18**

We're being conformed more and more to the image of Christ. And in the image of Christ, we see God's glory (see Col. 1:15). So as we become more like Christ through the Holy Spirit's work in our lives, we begin to reflect God's glory. Our character becomes more like God's. Our actions and reactions become more like His.

This transformation is a huge truth. Not only are we saved from sin, but we're also saved to Christlikeness. Though we're not perfect, we're being "transformed into the same image from one degree of glory to another" (2 Cor. 3:18), and one day "we shall be like him, *because we shall see him* as he is" (1 John 3:2, emphasis added).[3] On that last day, the true glory day, sin will no longer keep us from seeing God's glory or from glorifying Him.

THE GLORY OF BEING HUMAN

The Reformers believed there's something truly good about being a human, even though we're born sinful and with nothing good in us. We're broken. We're wanderers. Yet we're God's image bearers. And by grace alone through faith alone in Christ alone, we can become more like Christ "from one degree of glory to another" (2 Cor. 3:18).

Humanity is the pinnacle of God's creation, created to have a relationship with Him and to bear His image (see Gen. 1:27). In these respects we're different from dogs, owls, and sharks. We carry God's image. We're unique. Though sin mars the image, it doesn't destroy it. God can rejoice in His works—even us:

> May the glory of the LORD endure forever;
>   may the Lord rejoice in his works,
> who looks on the earth and it trembles,
>   who touches the mountains and they smoke!
> I will sing to the LORD as long as I live;
>   I will sing praise to my God while I have being.
> May my meditation be pleasing to him,
>   for I rejoice in the LORD.
> **PSALM 134:31-34**

We're not God, but through Christ we can be more and more like Him. We can freely rejoice in the Lord. Our glory days are ahead of us, and we can rightly give God the glory alone for that good news.

Spend the next few moments asking God to help you see His glory in every nook and cranny of life. Then tell Him ways you'll start giving Him glory instead of stealing it from Him.

1. Westminster Shorter Catechism, Westminster Shorter Catechism Project [online], 30 July 2016 [cited 9 November 2016]. Available from the Internet: *shortercatechism.com*.
2. John Calvin, as quoted in Michael Reeves and Tim Chester, *Why the Reformation Still Matters* (Wheaton, IL: Crossway, 2016), 211.
3. Ibid., 209.

GOSPEL APPLICATION

I will constrain no one by force, for faith
must come freely without compulsion.[1]
MARTIN LUTHER

It didn't take long for my daughter to start bending the rules. Her progression of obedience went from doing whatever I asked, to looking me in the eye while not doing whatever I asked, to looking for loopholes in whatever I asked. At first her obedience was a sort of blind trust. Then she began experimenting with what she could get away with before she got in trouble. Now her obedience is more clever; it's about doing whatever I ask but only enough to get by.

The Reformers weren't interested in teaching blind obedience or helping people find the line between obedience and disobedience. The works-based system of the Roman Catholic Church gave people ample reasons to try and cheat the system to find a way to salvation. The Reformers insisted that additives and substitutes weren't an option.

When it comes to Christian belief, we can't look for loopholes. And when we share the gospel with others, we can't offer loopholes that tell them what they want to hear. God doesn't receive glory from sales tricks; He receives glory from willing hearts that freely come to Him in worship. God's glory alone is beautiful; it doesn't need to be enhanced.

Reflect on what you've read about God's glory this week and list three reasons God's glory alone is crucial to Christian living.
1.

2.

3.

ALONE MEANS ALONE

In the previous lesson we learned that God created us for His glory and that salvation is for God's glory alone. In Exodus 14:18 God said He would save His people from slavery so that "the Egyptians shall know that I am the LORD, when I have gotten glory over Pharaoh, his chariots, and his horsemen." God saves us because He loves us but, more than that, because He wants His glory to be clearly seen.

This is precisely why the Reformers fought for the idea of God's glory alone. These words by Luther were made in response to someone's claim that works played a part in salvation:

> It is that once apparent from the look of their works that they did it all for their own glory, so that they were not ashamed to acknowledge and to boast that it was their own glory that they sought.[2]
>
> **MARTIN LUTHER**

If we can't boast (see Eph. 2:8-9), then salvation must be by grace alone through faith alone in Christ alone. Anything that involves human effort steals glory from God. Again and again, the Reformers fought for that word *alone* to really mean alone.

In contrast, the Roman Catholic Church glorified people (the pope, priests, dead saints, and so on). This disagreement wasn't merely about theological terms. It was about worshiping God rightly. If we were created to glorify Him, and if everything we do is for His glory (see 1 Cor. 10:31), then we don't have much room to glorify others or ourselves.

Again, as the Westminster Catechism says, we exist to glorify God and enjoy Him forever. The gospel is from God, and it's about God. In Luther's 95 Theses he said, "The true treasure of the church is the most holy gospel of the glory and grace of God."[3] We received the gospel in order to worship our Creator—to recognize and exalt His grace and glory.

In what ways do you treat the gospel as though it's about your glory instead of God's?

Why is the gospel about God and not us?

GOD'S GLORY TO THE END OF THE EARTH

We've read this passage a few times throughout this study, but we can't read it enough:

> *Jesus came and said to them, "All authority in heaven and on earth has been given to me. Go therefore and make disciples of all nations, baptizing them in the name of the Father and of the Son and of the Holy Spirit, teaching them to observe all that I have commanded you. And behold, I am with you always, to the end of the age."*
> **MATTHEW 28:18-20**

These were Jesus' final words and perhaps the most important words He said during His rescue mission on earth. Jesus has authority—ultimate authority—to save people. We go and make disciples because of His authority. This means we can never take credit for our salvation or the salvation of others. God's glory is seen when people worship Him alone.

Back in Genesis 1 the first people received a clear command from God immediately after they were created:

> *God said, "Let us make man in our image, after our likeness. And let them have dominion over the fish of the sea and over the birds of the heavens and over the livestock and over all the earth and over every creeping thing that creeps on the earth."*
> *So God created man in his own image,*
> *in the image of God he created him;*
> *male and female he created them.*
> *And God blessed them. And God said to them, "Be fruitful and multiply and fill the earth and subdue it, and have dominion over the fish of the sea and over the birds of the heavens and over every*

living thing that moves on the earth." And God said, "Behold, I have given you every plant yielding seed that is on the face of all the earth, and every tree with seed in its fruit. You shall have them for food. And to every beast of the earth and to every bird of the heavens and to everything that creeps on the earth, everything that has the breath of life, I have given every green plant for food." And it was so. And God saw everything that he had made, and behold, it was very good.
GENESIS 1:26-31

God gave Adam and Eve the task to "be fruitful and multiply" (v. 28). This command wasn't simply about procreation but about spreading God's image around the globe. He wanted people glorifying Him everywhere. Remember, we're created to glorify Him. The more people worship Him, the more His glory is made evident.

So in the Great Commission Jesus was simply telling us to follow the mission our ancient parents were first given: go and make more God-worshipers. Point them to His glory and let Him do the work. By grace alone through faith alone in Christ alone, God alone will receive glory.

How do we radiate God's glory when we carry out the Great Commission?

Why does God use us to help spread His glory around the globe?

POINTING TO GOD'S GLORY

We live in a human-centered world. Everyone everywhere, including us, cares more about themselves than they care about anyone else. We love and serve ourselves exactly the way we want to be loved and served. Maybe that's why Jesus told us to love others the way we love ourselves.

If we care for others the way we care for ourselves, chances are that we'll serve them well. But Jesus didn't want us to be selfish; He wanted us to be sacrificial and think of others first.

Unfortunately, the human-centered focus of our world creeps into the church. Sunday mornings are often about what the church can do for us, not what we can do for the church. We want to be fed or encouraged, but we're not as concerned with worshiping God or serving others. But Scripture tells us everything is for God's glory, and nothing else can compare to it.

In what ways is the world human-centered instead of God-centered?

In what ways is the church human-centered instead of God-centered?

List three people in your life who need to know about God's glory.
1.

2.

3.

We're called not to be human-centered but God-centered. We point away from ourselves. It's not about us. The Church in Luther's day sadly missed this foundational truth, making salvation about itself or at least through itself.

So even as we implement Jesus' command to make disciples of all nations, we have to keep in mind the idea of *alone*. We can't preach works-based salvation about getting cleaned up or trying harder. We can't point people to themselves, making salvation about their glory instead of God's glory. If we tell people salvation is all about them, they'll make Christianity human-centered. They'll be right back in the place from which Luther and the Reformers fought so hard to move believers away.

GOD ALONE

Telling people about God's glory seems like a daunting task. How can people in a human-centered world respond to a God-centered faith? Only by grace alone through faith alone in Christ alone, found in Scripture alone. Remember, salvation isn't about us, so saving people isn't about us.

The Holy Spirit was given to us to empower our mission to make disciples of all nations. Even our evangelism is powered by the Holy Spirit, under the authority of Jesus, pointing to the Father. We're merely the messengers of the greatest news ever told.

How has this study of the Reformation changed the way you view God and the gospel?

Spend the next few moments asking God how you can point the world to His glory and not to your own. Confess the ways you've made your life's purpose about you and acknowledge the ways you'll now make it about Him.

1. Martin Luther, as quoted in *Acts*, ed. Esther Chung-Kim and Todd R. Hains, vol. 6 in Reformation Commentary on Scripture, gen. ed. Timothy George (Downers Grove, IL: InterVarsity, 2014), 246.
2. Martin Luther, *The Bondage of the Will*, trans. J. I. Packer and O. R. Johnston (Grand Rapids, MI: Revell, 1957), 251–52.
3. Martin Luther, as quoted in Timothy J. Wengert, *Martin Luther's 95 Theses: With Introduction, Commentary, and Study Guide* (Minneapolis: Fortress, 2015), 22.

THE GOSPEL COALITION

is a broadly reformed network of churches with a passionate commitment to the gospel and its transforming power. We at LifeWay have partnered with The Gospel Coalition to offer several resources to strengthen and equip the church.

PRAYING WITH PAUL ■ by D.A. Carson and Brian Tabb

The apostle Paul found the kind of spiritual closeness in his own fellowship with the Father that is available to all of us. *Praying with Paul* leads group members into the Epistles to see what Paul taught in his "school of prayer." Group members will be exposed to the priorities of prayer, a God-centered framework for prayer, and practices for a more meaningful and dynamic prayer life. (8 sessions)

| Bible Study Kit | 005644096 | $59.99 |
| Bible Study Book | 005644095 | $12.99 |

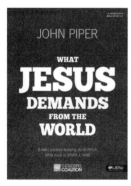

WHAT JESUS DEMANDS
FROM THE WORLD ■ by John Piper

The four Gospels are filled with demands from Jesus. They are not harsh demands originating from a selfish desire to control but rather loving directions for our ultimate satisfaction. This study serves as an accessible introduction for thoughtful inquirers and new believers, as well as a refreshing reminder for more mature believers of God's plan for His Son's glory and our good. (6 sessions)

| Bible Study Kit | 005644091 | $59.99 |
| Bible Study Book | 005644090 | $12.99 |

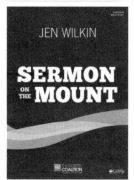

SERMON ON THE MOUNT ■ by Jen Wilkin

What does it mean to be a citizen of the kingdom of Heaven? Matthew's Gospel opens with three chapters containing Jesus' longest recorded message—a sermon given to His disciples early in His ministry to articulate what the life of a Christ-follower would look like. (9 sessions)

| Bible Study Kit | 005644877 | $59.99 |
| Bible Study Book | 005644876 | $12.99 |

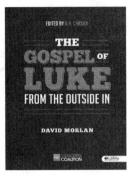

THE GOSPEL OF LUKE ■ by David Morlan

From start to finish of his Gospel, Luke depicts Jesus as accessible to the unknowns, the outcast, the lost, and the hopeless. But Luke points out that Jesus' desire was not just to call sinners but to call sinners to repentance. (12 sessions)

Bible Study Kit   005558731 $59.99
Bible Study Book   005558760 $12.99

1 PETER ■ by Jen Wilkin

Our inheritance through Christ is imperishable, undefiled, and unfading. In 1 Peter, a man of faith and flaws and eyewitness to the life of Christ challenges us to look beyond our current circumstances to a future inheritance. (9 sessions)

Bible Study Kit   005772640 $59.99
Bible Study Book   005772639 $12.99

MISSIONAL MOTHERHOOD ■ by Gloria Furman

God has instilled motherhood with meaning and purpose as part of His greater plan for humanity. Whether or not a woman has been called to traditional motherhood, she demonstrates her nurturing gifts daily through caregiving, hospitality, discipleship, teaching, raising children, and serving others. (6 sessions)

Bible Study Kit   006101513 $69.99
Bible Study Book   006101512 $12.99

REBUILD ■ by Kathleen Nielson with D.A. Carson

Taking a close look at the Book of Nehemiah, this study opens a window into the dramatic story of God's people sustained by God's Word. It points groups to God's sovereign plan to work through His people. (8 sessions)

Bible Study Kit   005644873 $59.99
Bible Study Book   005644872 $12.99

WHERE TO GO FROM HERE

We hope you enjoyed *Echoes of the Reformation*. If so, please share it on social media with #EchoesoftheReformation. And now that you've completed this study, here are a few possible directions you can go for your next one.

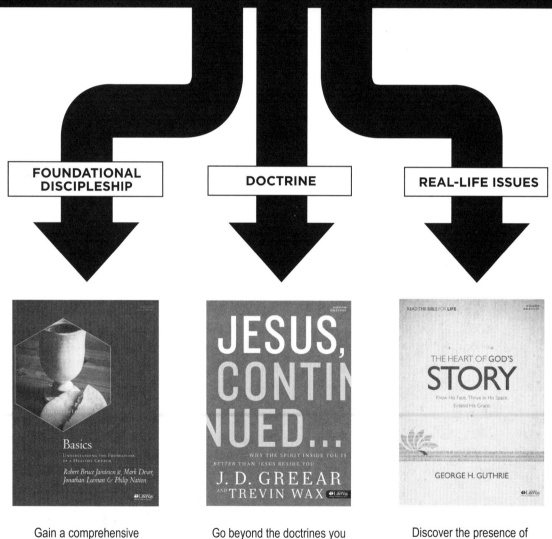

FOUNDATIONAL DISCIPLESHIP

Gain a comprehensive and rich understanding of the church and the way its components work together for effective, transformative ministry. (6 sessions)

DOCTRINE

Go beyond the doctrines you already know to the person Jesus wants you to know. (8 sessions)

REAL-LIFE ISSUES

Discover the presence of God at the heart of His story and understand why we were created, where we are heading, and how to live out God's gospel for the world in the present. (6 sessions)